Featherhood

A Memoir of Two Fathers and a Magpie

Charlie Gilmour

Scribner
New York London Toronto Sydney New Delhi

Scribner
An Imprint of Simon & Schuster, Inc.
1230 Avenue of the Americas
New York, NY 10020

First Scribner hardcover edition January 2021

Interior design by Wendy Blum

Manufactured in the United States of America

1 3 5 7 9 10 8 6 4 2

Library of Congress Cataloging-in-Publication Data is available.

ISBN 978-1-5011-9850-2
ISBN 978-1-5011-9852-6 (ebook)

For Olga

The eye that mocketh at his father, and despiseth to obey his mother, the ravens of the valley shall pick it out, and the young eagles shall eat it.

—Proverbs 30:17

Prologue

Somewhere in southeast London a flightless young magpie tumbles to the ground.

From below, it's hard to make out exactly where the bird dropped from. Its nest could have been high up in one of the plane trees that line this wheel-worn road, a bush-like bower hidden behind a green veil of leaves. Or it might have been tucked away somewhere in the jumble of semi-disused warehouses that clutter the area, an intricate formation of sticks and mud on corrugated iron and asbestos. Magpies construct their homes alongside ours, within sight but just out of reach. A magpie city superimposed on our own.

It is a harsh and very human environment into which this bird has prematurely arrived. Cars with crumpled fenders and shattered windshields wait in lines to be scrapped at the nearby junkyard. Illegally dumped fridges and sacks of rubble as immovable as boulders block the sidewalks. Puddles of spring rain shine purple with petrochemicals and, overhead, clouds of smoke and steam billow from the chimney of a huge waste-disposal facility that incinerates garbage around the clock. Trucks rumble past like thunderclouds and fans at the nearby soccer stadium roar. The only animals I've ever noticed there are pit bulls and rats, although a little farther afield, around the dump, there are flocks of gulls and pigeons along with a fleet of raptors sleek as fighter jets that are employed by the waste-disposal company to chase the other birds away.

My partner Yana's workshop is just around the corner, in a leaky industrial unit on the edge of the junkyard. This part of the city seems to be full of secrets and surprises, but they're rarely cute and fluffy. A police raid on a neighboring warehouse uncovers a cannabis farm one week; stolen motorbikes the next; a friend opens up a long-abandoned shipping container and finds it crammed full of Jet Skis; someone I once shared a prison cell with boasted of having dumped someone's sawn-off limbs nearby. This is the last place on earth I would have expected something as yolky soft and bird-bone brittle as a chick to turn up.

The creature scuttles around in the gutter, lurching toward the curb like a drunk staggering down an alleyway. Magpies leave home far too soon—long before they can really fly or properly fend for themselves. For weeks after they fledge their nests, they're dependent on their parents for sustenance, protection, and an education too. But this bird's parents are nowhere to be seen. They're not feeding it, or watching it, or guarding it; no alarm calls sound as a large apex predator approaches with footfalls made heavy by steel toe–capped boots. That doesn't mean the chick's parents aren't nearby. It could be no accident that this bird is on the ground. If food was running short, a savage calculation may have been performed, showing that the only way to keep the family airborne was to jettison the runt.

The magpie has stopped moving now. The black-and-white bird crouches down in the gutter, shivering from dehydration and perhaps fear too. If nature is allowed to run its course, it'll probably be dead before the day is out. The advancing human looms large as a tree trunk, sways uncertainly, and then, with a soft rustling, the bird's world goes dark.

A couple of hundred miles to the west, and three decades distant in time, a young jackdaw tumbled from its nest in the steeple of a village church. Steely-gray feathers, yellow beak, injured wing dragging along the ground. Jackdaws and magpies share family ties. The crow family. Carrion kin. Someone, perhaps the vicar, stumbled across this injured young bird, boxed it up, and took it to the home of a local woman, an amateur animal healer. From there, the jackdaw found its way into the hands of the man who would go on to become my father. The magpie finds its way to me.

PIN FEATHERS

Chapter 1

Yana sets the cardboard box, with its precious contents, very gently down on our bedroom floor. Her sister found it this morning, she explains, and picked it up and brought it to their workshop. In between hammering and drilling they've been feeding it live grubs from the angling supplier. The grubs bite, Yana continues matter-of-factly, so you have to crush their heads a little with pliers or a fingernail before sending them down the bird's hatch. She raises the flaps of the box.

A black-and-white ball of fluff the size of a child's fist is curled up in a corner. It looks dead. It smells dead. I click my tongue at the creature and one of its eyelids flutters open. Its eye is mineral blue.

I try to call to mind everything I know about magpies. At first, all I can come up with is the nursery rhyme "One for sorrow" and an image of my mum religiously saluting any she encountered on the farm I grew up on, to ward off the bad luck they're supposed to bring. Better safe than sorry, I think, touching my hand to the side of my head as I peer down into the box. Yana says they're clever birds—very clever, as all members of the crow family are—although I seem to recall that they're widely disliked for reasons I've never quite understood. Something about them eating baby songbirds and consorting with the devil. And they're said to have a pirate's eye for stolen treasure—a lost wedding ring should be looked for in the nearest magpie nest. Other than saluting it, I have no idea what you're meant to do with one. I've cared for injured wildlife before in a vague sort of way, or at least I tried to as a kid: creatures the cat dragged in, broken squirrels, birds that had jerked their brains to jelly against windowpanes. No matter what you do, it seems like they always end up in the same place: a shoebox at the bottom of a shallow grave. Even healthy animals haven't had the best of luck in my hands. I think guiltily of the beautiful white doves we had years ago, which my grandmother, my mother, and I dyed pastel pink and released on the farm—only for them to be gobbled up by the fox like so much cotton candy. If I'd been the one to come across this bird, I suspect I might have been tempted to let it take its chances down in the gutter. I'm not sure what we can do for it, except perhaps prolong its suffering.

I look from the bird to Yana. She's dressed, as usual for a workday, in a dark blue, paint-spattered coverall and heavy boots. Her light brown hair is held tightly in place with pins in a precise and severe style that adds a few grades of sharpness to her high and prominent cheekbones. She's already busy with the pliers. I watch as she goes snapping after a writhing yellow grub with her metallic beak and clamps down on its head. Pale goo oozes from both ends of the unfortunate grub as she waves it enticingly above the baby magpie. This is typical behavior. Yana is incapable of encountering a broken object without wanting to pick it up and make it better. I suppose she's something of a magpie herself: not a thief, exactly, but certainly a hoarder of found treasure. She always has a screwdriver at hand and rarely seems to think twice about dragging abandoned light fixtures, or slabs of marble, or enormous sacks of rocks that she's collected from the foreshore of the Thames back to our house. Our home is filled with things she's made or fixed: from shelves, to mugs, to knives, to the chairs we sit on and the trousers I wear. She takes special delight in suspending things from the ceiling. In the living room, a chandelier she made from sharp glass stalactites rattles whenever large vehicles go past; above our bed a framework of bamboo and string and trailing vines has turned our room into a jungle. She attributes her DIY attitude to having grown up as one of six siblings in a busy immigrant family. Her parents fled to Sweden from Soviet Ukraine with their children and whatever else they could carry, leaving the USSR to collapse behind them. It was a chaotic environment and having the ability to make your own clothes as well as your own fun came at a premium.

I first met her two years ago at a party in a disused carwash in Lewisham. She appeared from behind a concrete pillar with peroxide-blond hair and demonic-red eye makeup and hooked me with a glance. Later, she took me back to her place and showed me her albino snake, her orchid mantis, and her collection of homemade knives. Not long after that we moved in together and were swiftly engaged. It's all been very sudden, so much so that I'm slightly unsure as to how I've arrived at this point. At times I feel a little like one of her found objects. I certainly never imagined myself settling down in my twenties. Last time I checked, I had a shaved head, bruised knuckles, and was heading for a fall. Now I seem to be getting married, making a nest. Sometimes I'm convinced I've dreamt all this up, and everything could vanish as easily as waking. At other times, the opposite seems true: that I'm slowly regaining consciousness after a long and tiring nightmare. I don't know if it was Yana's willingness to take on the defective that drew her to me—I somehow doubt it. But her strength, solidity, invulnerability were certainly some of the qualities that pulled me to her.

Now this bad-luck bird has arrived. A dream-thing regarding Yana's dying worm suspiciously from its corner of the box. Both of its eyes are open now. Blue. I never knew that a young magpie's eyes were blue. All the magpies I've seen in the past, chattering in trees, or picking apart carcasses on roadsides, must have been adults, their eyes glinting obsidian. Though this bird's eyes are fully unshuttered, its sharp black beak remains stubbornly closed, no matter how Yana tries to tempt it. She mutters something under her breath that sounds like "stupid magpie" and sets her pliers down. Fixing this broken little crow might, I suspect, be beyond even her powers of repair.

"Isn't there someone else who can deal with this?" I say. "Like, I don't know, a vet?"

Yana rolls her eyes at me as if I'd just suggested hiring an electrician to come and change a lightbulb. Which is, to be fair, exactly the sort of thing I might try to do—for the lightbulb's sake. If Yana represents order, then I am chaos. Things just seem to fall apart in my hands, and this bird is all too breakable.

Yana waves me away and picks up the pliers again. She crushes a fresh worm and makes another pass at the magpie, this time emitting odd high-pitched chirruping noises and clacking her metal beak—just like, she claims, a mother magpie would do in the wild. With a sudden burst of energy, the bird's beak springs open and it begins to whistle like a kettle on the boil. Yana drops the worm into the bird's bright pink maw and in a single gulp it's gone. Clearly there's some life in the creature yet.

Yana passes me a grub from the plastic box in her tool bag. "Your turn," she says as the grub pulsates across the surface of my palm, yellow and faintly hairy, like a severed toe spasming away. I use the pliers to crush its head and then play mother. Reliable as a clockwork cuckoo, the bird opens wide. Its fragility terrifies me. Bone china with a feather boa. I gingerly set the reflexively squirming grub into its beak and wait for it to start chomping, but instead the bird just carries on screaming and the grub rolls out.

"You have to really shove it in," says Yana, stabbing at the air with her index finger.

I abandon the pliers. I can't bear to use such a hard metal implement on something so soft and delicate. I push the grub toward the rim of the bird's black throat with the tip of my finger instead. The bird's squealing intensifies, and then morphs into a sort of gremlin-like *yum-yum* as peristalsis kicks in and the worm is taken down below. The bird doesn't stop there. I feel the strong, circular muscles of its esophagus convulse against the end of my finger as it tries to swallow me too. I swiftly withdraw my hand. The bird chirps, tucks its head beside its wing, and falls back to sleep.

"What now?" I say.

"Get more worms," Yana says. "I think we'll have to feed it every twenty minutes and we're already running out."

Chapter 2

Over the next couple of days, I try as best I can to ignore the magpie in the box. I'm more convinced than ever that it's destined for an early grave. Yana has spotted some sort of parasite living in its throat and it has regular seizures; horrible, heartrending episodes where it throws itself onto its side and convulses like a frog that's been hooked up to the grid. Yana's problem, I decide. She sobs when these seizures strike and drips water from her fingertip into the corner of the bird's beak, which somehow revives it, although another attack always seems to be just around the corner. I suspect this was why it was thrown out of the nest in the first place. Birds know when one of their brood isn't worth bothering with. I write it off too. No point getting attached to something that isn't going to stick around.

And besides, I have a sneaking suspicion that Yana is trying to edge me into the role of magpie father. It's only natural, I suppose. Yana's work as a set designer often takes her away for days at a time. Whereas I'm an underemployed writer and, these days, I very rarely leave home at all. Bunker mentality—although the outside still seems to have managed to flap its way in. Should the creature survive, it seems almost inevitable that the role of chief worm crusher will eventually fall to me. If it makes it past this turbulent patch, it's obvious that it's going to need a lot of care before it can be sent back into the wild. It can't even feed itself; and flying seems like a distant dream. Who knows how long it will take to learn?

I attempt to feign disinterest as Yana tends to the creature, although it's hard not to get sucked in. She has her work cut out just keeping its belly full. She kills endless worms, rolls warm lamb mince into tiny magpie meatballs, softens dog biscuits in warm water and funnels them into the bird. I don't know how she knows how to do all this stuff, but it seems to be working. The magpie's life still seems far from certain—it's barely strong enough to support the minuscule weight of its own head and it still shakes and convulses horribly—but under Yana's protective wing the frequency of its fits is lessening. The bird's blue eyes stay open for longer periods of time, and they follow Yana and me hungrily around the room.

A few days later, the inevitable happens. Yana's agent calls to say that a lucrative job has come up at short notice—in Paris. Yana wipes the meat juice from her hands, zips up her coverall, and is out the door with her tool bag slung over her shoulder in the blink of a magpie's eye. Back in a week, she says as she leaves.

I stare down at the bird. The bird stares steadily back at me, angling its head sideways and up so it has me right in the barrel of its black pinprick pupil. I can't quite escape the feeling that there is an intelligence lurking behind those pale gemstone eyes, an intelligence that is scrutinizing me just as intensely as I am it. I've never felt so seen by an animal. I worry that this is not going to go well. I am clumsy, absentminded, and a serial shirker of responsibility. The magpie is rapidly becoming as demanding and unreasonable as a toddler in a candy shop—but is still as delicate as spun sugar.

Alone with the bird, I turn to my computer to try to find out more about what you're meant to do with a creature like this. I don't have much luck. There's a lot of practical information out there but, on first look, all of it seems to concern the killing of magpies rather than their preservation. There are pages and pages of discussions on pest-control blogs and air rifle enthusiasts' forums about how to lure and shoot or trap these birds. Hobby hunters sucker them down into their back gardens with bits of meat and then blast their brains out with lead pellets. They post pictures boasting of their kills: adult magpies tossed on the floor like oily rags, their iridescent feathers wet with blood. The hatred I discover online makes me immediately take the magpie's side.

As to why they're so hated, I can't quite get to the bottom of it. The way people talk about them murdering songbirds suggests they're personally responsible for the collapse of the ecosystem. It does seem to be true that magpies are opportunistic predators who sometimes eat the eggs and chicks of other birds—but then why aren't kestrels, buzzards, sparrow hawks, owls, cats, and, most of all, humans hated and hunted with equal fervor? The further I look into the alleged crimes of magpies, the less sense they make. They're said to tear out the eyes, tongues, and anuses of lambs. They keep a spot of the devil's blood under their tongue. They alone of all the birds refused to mourn for Christ. They cackled madly from the rigging of Noah's ark as civilizations sank. The very word *magpie* seems to be loaded with ancient scorn, deriving from the Old English *mag*, a derogatory word for a gossiping woman, a reference to the bird's rough chatter, although it seems to be the magpies themselves who have been the victims of gossip. Perhaps the hatred humans seem to feel toward them has something to do with their supposed supernatural powers. Magpies can apparently bring luck, good and bad; they can predict the future; they can tell of death and birth. Everyone knows the rhyme, or a version of it: One magpie brings sorrow; two mirth; three a wedding; four a birth; five silver; six gold; and seven the devil, his own self.

All of this is very interesting, but it's not *terribly* useful, so I pick up my phone and call my grandmother for advice instead. At various points in her colorful life she's been a soldier in Chairman Mao's Red Army; an announcer for Radio Peking; a translator for the Chinese state propaganda department; and, most improbably of all to those who know her, a headmistress at a village school in Devon. She's had more husbands than I can name, but the one constant in her life seems to be animals. She's kept house geese, goats, bred Staffordshire bull terriers, had a pet monkey that used to secretly pee in people's coffee. And then there was the sparrow she rescued, presumably at great personal risk, during Mao's campaign against the birds, like some sort of Communist Dr. Dolittle. The Smash Sparrows Campaign was a feather-brained attempt to prevent crops from being lost to thieving beaks by exterminating the species. Sparrows were frightened into the air and kept there with drums, rattles, and firecrackers, until they collapsed from exhaustion. Dying sparrows piled up in the streets of Peking like drifts of snow. It was one of these creatures that my grandmother picked up and secretly nurtured. She's a tough old bird herself—I pity the thug who tries to jump her on pension day—but she's a caring one too.

"A magpie?" she squawks. "What do you want to keep one of those alive for? Horrible creatures. Why don't you drown it instead?"

Ah, I think. I've inadvertently stumbled across one of my grandmother's many inexplicable pet peeves. They often seem to be animal based, come to think of it: the natural world subjected to a private logic of good and bad that, from the outside, doesn't necessarily make a lot of sense. The fat, one-eyed rat that scrabbles beneath the boards of her conservatory is a source of great delight, but the wood pigeons, cooing happily from a branch in her neighbor's garden, are evil. So, it seems, are magpies. I listen as she tells me about how the pair nesting in the tree above her little cottage in a quiet corner of North London have been driving her up the wall with their mad cackling. She suspects they're planning on eating her little robin and wants to know if I can get her a pistol, preferably one with a silencer.

I try my mum next, hoping for better luck as the number rings. She grew up in a zoo of my grandmother's making and, from the way she tells it, it's always sounded like the responsibility for the other inmates generally fell to her. Whenever Blodwin the nanny goat got away and ran into the village to feast on people's flower beds, she'd be the one to have to go and haul her back. When feathers flew between the foul-tempered geese, she'd be sent shouting and flapping into the yard to split them up. As the only daughter of a head teacher and an overworked Communist journalist in a house in the middle of nowhere, she was probably glad for the company, although as soon as she'd saved up enough money she bought a wild pony from an Irish Traveller for a song and rode away from the zoo as long and hard as she could.

She laughs when I tell her about her mum's advice.

"The person you should really be talking to about this is your father," she says. "Your biological father, I mean. He had a tame bird just like it. Well, not a magpie; a jackdaw, I think it was—but they're the same family, aren't they? I'm pretty sure he wrote a poem about it. And there's a picture somewhere too, I think."

This is not the answer I was expecting. It's not an entirely welcome revelation either, although I have little trouble believing it to be true. It's just another fantastical detail to add to the confusing and contradictory portrait I have of the man who gave me life and then flew away. Most of the information I have about my biological father is secondhand: from my mum and from the Internet. I couldn't tell you how he takes his tea, or what sort of music he likes, but I can give you some of the obvious highlights, only slightly more than what is on his Wikipedia page. Heathcote Williams (b. 1941): squatter, writer, actor, alcoholic, poet, anarchist, magician, revolutionary, and Old Etonian. A wild-haired icon of the radical sixties underground whose plays and essays rode the twin currents of psychedelia and sex. From a distance, he's always seemed like a man possessed of powerful magic, able to break rules at will. He once took control of several streets in West London, opened the houses to the homeless, and then declared independence from the United Kingdom—although not, so the story goes, before having himself crowned mayor. Something of the gentleman thief about him, he once used his conjuring abilities to steal Christmas from Harrods, turkey and all. He could juggle fire, breathe fire even, although perhaps hasn't since he self-immolated on a girlfriend's doorstep. Passionate about animals, he once shat into his hand and threw his excrement at a Dutch performance artist who was about to have sex with a live goose, and then ran away with the goose. Master of the vanishing act, he disappeared in the dead of night when I was six months old, without warning and without explanation. And he had a tame jackdaw that rode around on his shoulder like a pirate with a parrot—why not?

I press my mum for more information about Heathcote's relationship with this jackdaw but she can only be vague. She thinks the bird was around just before they met and had me, almost thirty years ago now. That at least places the jackdaw at Port Eliot, the stately home in Cornwall where Heathcote lived at the invitation of his old school friend, Lord Peregrine Eliot, for over a decade. My mum and I lived there for a little while too, in a pig farmer's cottage in the woods that Heathcote had been lent by Peregrine—a happy family among the trees, at least until Heathcote broke down.

"Yes, Port Eliot. That must be right," my mum says. Peregrine, she recalls, was full of unwelcome jokes about how Heathcote had got himself a new "dirty bird" to play with when she arrived on the scene.

"But don't let that put you off," she says, as if she can hear me wrinkling my nose on the other end of the line. "Why don't you read the poem. Or better yet, ask Heathcote."

I don't read the poem and I don't ask Heathcote. There was a time when a coincidence like this would have delighted me. I'd have seen it as proof of our connection. And an opportunity for us to bond. But I've been burned too many times since for me to seriously consider thoughts like that. Each time I've reached out to grab hold of Heathcote, he's vanished like smoke. First when I was twelve, then seventeen, and then twenty, each disappearance more upsetting than the last. After all that, I vowed I'd never make the mistake of reaching out to him again; except I'm not sure if I really learned my lesson, because I recently sent him an invitation to my wedding, and I have a childish hope that he might come. These days we email, but our relationship is complicated, to say the least. We talk, but we don't really communicate. He makes gestures: sends me his new books of poetry, signs his cards "Dad," with a kiss, as if he believes that by doing so he can magically overwrite the last twenty-seven years of absence without the need for any difficult apologies or explanations. I, for my part, seem completely unable to express my feelings to him. We're both stuck. And the gap this has created between his version of reality and mine is jarring. Perhaps he was the perfect father to his jackdaw, but I'll be damned if I go to him for parenting advice.

I turn my attention back to the magpie instead. It doesn't seem to mind that I haven't been able to dig up any useful information. All it cares about is worms, and it seems willing to accept me as a supplier just as readily, just as greedily, as it did Yana. It is a box of appetite, a baby I don't remember asking for, one that flung itself from a branch and into my bedroom.

Chapter 3

Like the magpie, my mother and I fell to earth in the spring. It happened at night: a silent shove in the dark that reduced our nest to splinters. Heathcote never really explained what made him do it; why he vanished and why he then went so very mad. According to my mum, it came from nowhere, like lightning from a clear blue sky, like something lurking invisibly in the blood. This is what I know of our story; most of it comes from her.

My mum, Polly, was twenty-six when she met Heathcote. She'd left home at sixteen, moved to London, had a series of hopeless-sounding boyfriends, and got a job at a major publishing house, which, in the 1980s, was quite an achievement for a woman with no degree and no connections, never mind the Oxbridge qualifications her colleagues seemed incapable of shutting up about. Heathcote was one of her authors. In the 1960s, he'd been a promising young playwright and a counterculture figure with a minor cult following. Harold Pinter was a fan. But then he went off radar, for years it seemed. *Whale Nation*—a book-length poem celebrating the beauty and mourning the plight of the whale—was to be his return to the public eye and my mum was in charge of publicity.

Professional meetings soon became anything but: he would make silver dollars appear from the sugar bowl, showed her sleight of hand, and promised to teach her to juggle. They went on long walks and he sent magic tricks in the mail. Soon he was insisting that whenever he came up from his lodgings in Cornwall that she meet him off the sleeper train at dawn, and they'd breakfast together for hours at the Great Western Hotel. Heathcote was much older than her, well into his forties, but that didn't seem to matter. He was charmingly childlike: mischievous, playful, and funny. She enjoyed spending time with him, and they seemed to be spending more and more of it together.

There were one or two odd moments in their long and uncertain courtship. Despite all the letters and long chats over breakfast, Heathcote somehow didn't find a moment to mention that he had a family. He was, he told my mum, a hermit. So it was something of a surprise when Heathcote's two daughters, China and Lily, and their mother, Diana, showed up at a reading of *Whale Nation* at the National Theatre—even more so when Heathcote reacted by running out the door and diving into a taxi. That, perhaps, should have been a red flag; but, at that stage, he and my mum weren't even together, and later, when they were, he reassured her that he hadn't been with Diana for years. She lived in Oxford with the children; he in solitude in Cornwall. He wasn't lying when he'd said he was a hermit, but he wasn't exactly being fulsome with the truth either.

After the unexpected success of *Whale Nation*, Heathcote returned to what he described as his "garret" in Cornwall. He had another book to finish: *Falling for a Dolphin*. It was a love letter to a wild bottlenose that he'd spent weeks swimming with in the Irish Sea. It was a miraculous relationship; another magical episode in Heathcote's life. He would wade into the water, sink his face into the sea, shout "Dolphin!" into the brine, and the creature would arrive, a twelve-foot-long, sentient torpedo that bore him on its back to deserted coves, where it would dive for fish and share its catch with Heathcote. The poem, he later told my mum, was tangled up with his feelings for her, and it was on the tour for that book, in late 1988, that they finally got together. By spring of the next year, my mum was pregnant with me.

Heathcote already had a family and my mum was rather young. But Heathcote was, for once in his life, clear.

"You can't kill someone for bad timing," he said. "We would have ended up having a child anyway."

My mum's boss called her into his office when he found out she was going to keep the baby.

"I just wanted to congratulate you," he said with spectacularly misplaced confidence. "Heathcote will be the most marvelous father."

Port Eliot wasn't quite the hermitage Heathcote had made it out to be to my mum. He had effective control of an entire wing of his friend Peregrine's twelfth-century stately home and the housekeeper there delivered hot food to his door. Heathcote lived at the center of a labyrinth of books, papers, and news clippings, working obsessively on his meticulously researched poems during the day and sleeping in a den of filthy bedding at night. Too busy to go to the toilet, he filled whatever came to hand with piss. With a baby on the way, he and my mum began fixing up an old pig farmer's cottage in the woods. They sunk a well, planted walnut trees, did their best to turn it into a comfortable nest. My mum had all her furniture and books moved in. We were, she thought, in it for the long haul.

Aristocratic squalor aside, it was a golden time. Heathcote was fun to be with; fascinating and funny. With the *Falling for a Dol-*

phin tour still ongoing, my mum booked them into fancy hotels around the country. They threw juggling parties at my mum's place when they were in London, and when she was eight months pregnant Heathcote took her to Ireland to meet the dolphin. High on Guinness and Black, he asked her to marry him. "In vino veritas," he said, when she accused him of being drunk. True or not, they somehow never quite got round to it.

For my first six months, Heathcote was apparently a marvelous father, as predicted. When I woke up in the morning, he would be the one to get out of bed and deal with me, leaving my mum to sleep in. He was obsessed—long before organic food became a thing—with making chemical-free baby food. They both, somehow, found time and energy to write. My mum, having left publishing, was starting her career as a journalist. Heathcote carried on with his poetry, walking to Port Eliot every day to scribble away inside his paper maze. Winter melted into spring and the forest around our cottage teemed with life. Sometimes Heathcote returned from his trips to the big house with a pheasant given to him by the local hunt, and my mum would pick the shotgun pellets from its meat and mash it up for me. Perhaps Heathcote was the only one who knew how fragile the whole arrangement was. On the surface, everything seemed perfect; until, suddenly, it wasn't.

One afternoon that spring, he and my mum sat in the woods with me next to them on a carpet of bluebells. "This is more than I deserve," Heathcote said—and he must have meant it because the next day he was gone.

The morning everything changed, my mum was woken early by my crying. Heathcote's side of the bed was empty and cold, but he clearly wasn't with me. He wasn't downstairs either, or out in the yard. A nocturnal flight had taken place. Heathcote had faded into the forest wordless as an owl, leaving as much trace as a bird through an open window.

It turned out he hadn't flown very far—only a mile or so through the woods to the big house—but he might as well have been up in the treetops. He was beyond reach.

"He's having a breakdown and he doesn't want to see you," said Lord Eliot when my mum tracked him down. "You can't expect him to play mummy bear, daddy bear, and baby bear forever, you know."

After several failed attempts, tramping back and forth through the bluebells from the cottage to the house, my mum eventually managed to sneak in. Heathcote was indeed quite mad. His eyes were red and raw, his hair wilder than ever.

"I'm ill," he repeated, over and over again. "I'm ill. I'm ill. I'm ill."

My mum held me up to him.

"This is your medicine," she said.

"I'm ill," said Heathcote. "I'm ill. I'm ill. I'm ill."

We were ejected from the house. What had happened she could only guess; Heathcote never seemed to have thought he owed her much of an explanation. The months that followed were hard. My mum had nowhere she could really go. She tried her parents' home in Devon, but we couldn't stay there for long, and so back to Port Eliot we went.

In the meantime, Heathcote had discharged himself from the big house and we went back to living in the cottage as a family. Heathcote and my mum tried to make things work, but it was like Heathcote had been split in two. In person he would be loving—and deeply apologetic. But as soon as my mum went to London for work he would switch, calling her up and ranting madly and unpleasantly.

Heathcote seemed to have decided there wasn't room in his

life for both poetry and family. So, he began squeezing out the latter. There was one sentence he kept repeating, a well-known quote from the writer Cyril Connolly: "There is no more sombre enemy of good art than the pram in the hall."

Eventually, it all became too much. My mum moved back to London for good. Heathcote stayed in Cornwall. She knew the family dream was dead—but wanted her child to at least grow up knowing both of his parents.

"One day I'll see him," Heathcote said the last time they spoke. "One day. When I'm better. I'd like that."

Needless to say, that day was a long time coming. Over a decade, in fact. After the breakup, Heathcote cut me and my mum out of his life like a tumor. He didn't visit, didn't write, never sent a birthday card. Any sense memory I might have had of him—a pair of brown eyes looming above my crib, a deep voice, the comforting smell of familiar skin—faded silently away.

Chapter 4

In my own nest, the baby magpie seems to come more and more to life as the week goes on. Alone with the bird, my days take on a strange rhythm. At dawn the shrieking begins. I murder a worm. Twenty minutes later, shrieking again. More decapitated worms, raw mince, and horribly spongy dog kibble. I clean the grease from beneath my fingernails, sit at my computer to write, and the shrieking starts up again. With Yana gone, I dance to the magpie's tune, becoming more and more like a bird as I do. I catch flies from the air and tease grubs from the soil. I flit back and forth, bringing spiders, caterpillars, and wood lice to their deaths. Things go on in this way until dusk. I get nothing done, can barely leave the house, am somehow utterly exhausted before the week is out.

Soon the magpie begins throwing open its gunshot wound of a throat whenever it detects my presence near its box, as if it recognizes my transformation into father bird. Even the sound of my voice is enough to set it off. I watch, mesmerized, as it absorbs hundreds of tiny lives into its own, constructing skin, muscle, bone, complex feathers, and sharp talons from cartilaginous gunk. I find myself wondering if it even remembers its life in the trees, when its parents had licorice eyes, sharp black beaks, and spoke to it in chitters and squawks.

Long before Yana's week away is over the creature outgrows its box. It scrabbles energetically against the sides, insisting that I pick it up and allow it to explore the world of our bedroom with pattering steps and clumsy leaps. It runs top-heavy on its long thin legs, seemingly in constant danger of overbalancing as it races to investigate alluring plug sockets and serpentine electricity cables. It defecates at will.

I follow the magpie around with a new eye, making note of the pins and needles scattered across the floor from the wedding outfit Yana was in the middle of sewing before she left, the tube of superglue on her bedside table, and the bowie knife balanced on mine. Seen from a parent bird's perspective, our room—our whole home, in fact—is a death trap. There are things that no wild bird should ever have to worry about. Electricity. Doors to be crushed in. A toilet bowl to drown in. What happens if a nosy beak gets jammed in a toaster? Birds generally seem to be peculiarly sensitive to fumes, hence sending the canary down the coal mine, and the Internet tells me that cleaning products, aerosol cans, and the gases given off by nonstick frying pans are all deadly to birds. Things I leave lying around more casually than bleach seem to be fatal too: certain houseplants, avocados, onions, garlic, mushrooms, dried beans, and chocolate are all potential killers—of more common house birds like parrots and cockatoos at least.

As the magpie scuttles across the floor, I find myself again wishing I could compare notes with someone who has had actual experience in raising a bird like this. I scroll through the contacts on my phone, trying to think of someone else to call, but it's not exactly brimming with magpie owners. The only person I can think of is Heathcote, and I'm beginning to doubt even that. The more time I spend with this magpie, the less I believe in the existence of Heathcote's jackdaw. This creature is a lot of work. Mess. Noise. Constant feeding. A jackdaw would presumably be the same. They're from the same family of birds, after all: corvids, or the crow family. Heathcote couldn't even cope with tending to his own offspring for long. How he would have managed with a bird is beyond my understanding. The jackdaw is a riddle; but perhaps it's also a clue.

With some reluctance, I turn to the shelf where I keep Heathcote's books and pamphlets. There's his first book, *The Speakers*, written when he was barely out of his teenage years and had immersed himself in the precarious lives of the public orators of Hyde Park's Speakers' Corner. It's a piece of reportage part George Orwell, part Jean Genet, unflinching in its portrayal of drug use, mental illness, homelessness, and sex. It was critically acclaimed when it was released in 1964—words of praise from the likes of Anthony Burgess, William Burroughs, and Harold Pinter light up the cover—but like most of Heathcote's work, and like Heathcote himself, it seems to have faded into obscurity since. I walk my fingers past it, past the trinity of book-length animal poems—*Whale Nation*, *Falling for a Dolphin*, and *Sacred Elephant*—that gave him another unexpected burst of success around the time I was born. These three have been on my shelf wherever I've lived for as long as I can remember. At least one of them was a gift from Heathcote. His handwriting slopes across the inside cover of *Falling for a Dolphin*, telling me about how he took my mum to swim with the dolphin while she was pregnant with me, how the dolphin used its ultrasound to scan her belly and so was the first creature to catch sight of me. It's a letter from the past that has always niggled at me: How can such apparent happiness just vanish?

Next come Heathcote's more recent works. These I struggle with. In the year or so since we resumed contact, Heathcote has sent me most of them. Thin little books of poetry and pamphlets that arrive in the mail, and which I simply don't seem to be able to read. I try but my eyes just slide off the page and I have to give up, hence I've never come across his poem about the jackdaw before. I don't know why I have such an allergic reaction to the poems Heathcote sends. Perhaps it's because they're not the words I want; although it probably doesn't help that they just don't seem to be very good. I'm not alone in this evaluation. The Pinters and Burroughses of the day certainly aren't lining up to praise Heathcote's self-published ramblings about Diogenes of Sinope.

I locate the jackdaw poem in a slim blue paperback volume entitled *Forbidden Fruit: Meditations on Science, Technology, and Natural History.* This, I realize, is the first time I've actually opened this book. "Being Kept by a Jackdaw" is nestled between poems about bees and capitalism, wasp honey and the Falklands War, the suicide of Alan Turing and the abuse suffered by workers building computers in Chinese factories today. This time my eyes don't slide off the page. The jackdaw poem is rich, sensory, and unexpectedly tender. It begins with Heathcote at a country fair being lured into a tent by the sweet smell of tansy pancakes cooking on a brazier. Inside he finds birds: stacks of wooden cages containing injured birds. A raven called Aubrey hypnotizes him with its stare, and a boyhood dream he once had, of having a jackdaw as a friend, comes flashing back into his mind. In that tent, his boyhood dream comes to life. I have to read the poem several times before I can relax into it; then I sit down on the floor with the magpie beside me and fall through the pages into the old man's world.

Chapter 5

The raven's feathers slide over each other like carbon steel scales as it shifts on its perch, something serpentine about the way it fixes the new arrival in its glare, like a cobra or a moray eel hypnotizing its prey. With minute movements of its head, the raven absorbs Heathcote, taking in every detail, from the frayed ends of his shoelaces, to the leather patches at his elbows, the dirt under his fingernails, the wild bird's nest hair sticking from his head, and beyond, seeing him in frequencies and aspects outside the scope of human understanding. Heathcote's thin lips are parted in quiet awe; the bird is immaculate, godlike, an obsidian icon come to life.

Between them, the smoke from a burning brazier bruises the air, and a traveler couple, Dave and Di, bustle around it, making tea and cooking tansy pancakes on a greasy cast-iron skillet. "I see Aubrey has got you under his spell," says Di, offering the visitor a slightly grimy blue mug of sweet English tea.

The raven, recognizing its name, or perhaps finally pronouncing its judgment on the stranger, opens its ebony beak and croaks; a penetrating, almost alien noise that makes Heathcote's viscera itch. He blinks, takes the cup of tea, turns his attention to the human in front of him. She explains how Aubrey, like the other birds in the wooden cages stacked around them, came into her care, a broken thing that she and her partner, Dave, nursed back to health; how, even though the door to his cage is always open, Aubrey never flies away, not even on a day like today with all the temptations of a Cornish country fair in early summer swirling around them.

Heathcote's eyes widen in delight. Like the raven's, his eyes at first appear beetle black, but when the sun catches them at an angle, as it does now, they light up like varnished mahogany. He remembers a fantasy he had as a child. "Aubrey's eerie presence triggered an old boyhood dream / Of having a jackdaw on your shoulder, like a pirate. / Whispering secrets in your ear, this jackdaw would speak / In a language that only you could understand." A magical companion to talk to him, protect him.

Dave prepares Aubrey's supper: a raw duck's egg in the shell, biscuits soaked in blood, a day-old chick that weeps plasma from its eye, all piled up in a battered tin bowl. Aubrey croaks again, revealing a scarlet throat and a long, thin tongue. There is a wet crunching noise, like someone breaking the surface of a crème brûlée, as the bird penetrates the egg with a single thrust, scattering gooey shards of shell in its hunger for the yolk. I imagine Heathcote wrinkling his nose. In his boyhood fantasy, he'd surely never really imagined that a bird might have such grisly needs. But, as the sun begins to set, and Di throws a cloth over Aubrey's cage, he senses opportunity slipping away.

"Ever since childhood . . ." They looked patiently quizzical. "I've wanted . . . I've always wanted to look after a jackdaw," he blurts out, looking slightly shamefaced, as if he'd just revealed a dirty secret.

Dave Nelstrop said casually, "Oh, we've got one. A fledgling. It was too poorly to bring. It's being fed by a dripper. With touches of brandy. It just fell out of its nest in a bell tower." He looks at Di with a question in his eyes. She nods. They promise to bring it next time they happen by.

One week later, at dawn, Heathcote wakes with something hard and sharp forced between his lips. He stirs, groans, and the object is withdrawn. Blearily, he unsticks his eyelids and, from a distance of a few inches, a single, perfectly round, azure eye stares insanely down at him. Jack Daw, as the bird has been christened, reinserts its beak into Heathcote's mouth and, like a doctor with a speculum, prizes it open. Too tired to resist, Heathcote lies back in his pile of dirty bedding and allows his new companion, "searching for a morsel from last night's meal," to tease fragments of the previous evening's beef wellington from between his canines.

All it really needs, the Nelstrops had told him, is a bit of rest—but it seems they forgot to inform the jackdaw. It is, Heathcote thinks wearily, inexhaustible—"a dive-bombing comet of energy and appetite." Somehow he hadn't expected it to be quite this alive. "At close quarters its feral behavior was dominated by a consuming curiosity, but who was it exactly? This bird that had lived its life in a tower, then fallen, and whose cowl made it look like a hooded monk."

The bird hops off Heathcote's chest to start rooting around in his sheets, stained treasure-map yellow by dried sweat and spilled tea. Heathcote watches, amazed despite the unreasonable hour, as the bird busily turns over folds, plows furrows, jabs its beak into crevices. Dipping and bobbing its head like someone in frantic prayer. The jackdaw pauses. It's found something soft, pink, and hairy. It gives it a sharp pinch and Heathcote yowls. This is evidently not what the bird is looking for, because it marches back up to Heathcote's head and yowls right back at him.

Heathcote mutters and, like a marionette being jerked to life, collects his spindly limbs together and rises. He is naked—except, that is, for the jackdaw perched on his shoulder. As he catches sight of his reflection in the large curved window set in the wall of his rounded room he grins. Life hasn't worked out exactly as he fantasized forty-odd years ago, but this is pretty close. Without looking down, he opens his bladder and shoots a golden stream of piss into the mouth of a wide-necked vase. It is already three-quarters full and his new contribution pushes its foul contents right up to the rim. It is one of many such receptacles scattered around on the floor: saucepans, pint glasses, a crystal decanter, even an eighteenth-century chamber pot—that was the first to be filled. Soon the room will be unin-

habitable, Heathcote thinks ruefully, what with the bird's excrement to contend with too.

He looks out the window. He will miss this particular view. It is picture-postcard perfect: the eye rolls down the softly sculpted valley toward the River Tamar, its wide estuary already twinkling in the dawn, birds picking around in the mudflats, the railway line walking on stilts far above it. But, looking around at the growing mess, he doesn't see any other solution. It's lucky this wing of the house is virtually deserted: He can keep rolling down the corridor for years to come, shutting and sealing doors behind him as he goes.

He likes to think of himself as a squatter here. That's what he tells people he is doing, anyway, although the reality is that he is simply over-staying his welcome. When Peregrine said he could come and stay for a while he probably didn't expect him to still be here five years later, filling his Ming vases with human waste. Nor, most likely, did Heathcote's two daughters or their mother.

Heathcote pulls on some trousers and seats himself at his writing desk. The Work is the most important thing. That's why he came here: a place of peace, far from the confines of the "family sandwich," as he calls it, where he can be totally free to create.

From the surface of the desk, the obscenely annotated face of the prime minister, Margaret Thatcher, glowers up at him. He picks up his pen and is just about to strike a bold new line when the jackdaw shrieks at him again, right in his ear this time. He had somehow half forgotten that it was there. With its pink throat exposed so close to his face he feels like he can see all the way down into its empty belly. "Almost immediately I became the bird's captive, existing solely to attend its needs, wondering if I'd experience Stockholm syndrome, which means you fall in love with your captors."

Mealworms and milk: that's what the Nelstrops said it eats. As he hunts around for the bird's breakfast things, he wonders how, in nature, jackdaws would go about acquiring milk for their young. Perhaps they mob the milk truck, like seagulls after a fishing trawler. Or else they hop skip jump up to cows' udders and hang there like angry black clothespins until their throats are full. It strikes him that jackdaws might not really drink milk—but, nevertheless, he tips the carton into his only unpolluted pan and sets it to warm on his portable stove.

The bird leaps on the worms, scattering them across the floor in its hunger. A parting gift from the Nelstrops, they crawl slowly into the dark recesses between the floorboards and vanish. The jackdaw splashes its charcoal face in the bowl of warm milk.

Heathcote shrugs and returns to the chaos of his desk. He pushes Thatcher to one side, guiltily reburies a letter from his mother asking if he would like to send her any of his sweaters or socks for repair, and pulls a Moleskin notepad toward him. He starts to scribble. An idea he's been working on for a while is beginning to take shape: an epic poem about whales, something with the rhythm and power of an incantation, a protective spell that he will cast over them. His surroundings fade away until all that exists is the nib of his calligraphic pen scratching out runes on pearl-white paper.

The jackdaw is having none of it, "behaving like some tyrannical movie star, demanding full attention day and night." It hops from floor to knee to desk and strikes the pen with a mighty jackhammer blow that causes it to shoot an arterial spurt of dark ink across the page. Heathcote looks at his papers, trampled beneath the jackdaw's black feet, and starts to feel a little glum. He is, he realizes, a captive once again.

Chapter 6

The jackdaw's echo wakes me at sunrise. *How can this be?* I think, groggily, as I feel something hard and sharp probing the meat of my face. How did Heathcote put it? "A bony road-drill picking at your teeth." I open my eyes to see my tormentor standing imperiously on my sternum, just above my heart, examining me critically through a single milky-blue eye. The bird has learned to escape its box and leap up onto our bed and now seems to be impatient for its breakfast, or possibly thinks I am its breakfast. I try not to flinch as the bird tugs on my lower lip like a piece of elastic. These acts are not, I decide, meant badly. If the bird really wanted to dig into my flesh then it probably could: evidence of the damage its beak can do when used as a pickax is all around me.

I believe in Heathcote's jackdaw now. His poem is too carefully observed for it to have been a figment, and I've found photographic evidence online. The photo is small, grainy, not quite in focus, like a foggy memory. It shows a man seated in front of a large circular table in a cavernous room with his back to the camera. He has a great mane of dark, shaggy hair. It's unmistakably Heathcote. Both shoulders of his dark suit jacket are splashed white, and on the back of a chair to his left a steely-gray jackdaw perches, returning his gaze.

I reach under my pillow for my phone and take a picture of the bird standing so haughtily on my chest. Perhaps I will send an email to Heathcote after all.

In the two weeks it's been with us, the magpie has grown into quite a handsome fellow. There's something princely in the way he struts about the bed in his cape of black silk and snowy ermine fur, his nascent flight feathers flashing like jewels. Both Yana and I have started to think of the magpie as a male. We have nothing of real substance to base this on; magpies, like most members of the crow family, are impossible to sex on sight, as they possess no outwardly visible genitalia and do not display any particular difference in size or plumage either. But the bird has to be one or the other, and we've got a fifty percent chance of being right.

Beak glinting, the bird makes another lunge for my septum. This time I duck beneath the covers, feeling like a giant as he pads around on the duvet above me, talons pressing down as light as a kitten's paws.

As I get up to prepare the magpie's first meal of the day I think again about Heathcote and his bird. Moments like this morning—moments that seem like echoes transmitted across generations—are a little unsettling. Anything that makes it seem as if I'm following in Heathcote's footsteps sets alarm bells ringing. The last time I went chasing after his shadow, it led me to a breakdown of my own, and these days I have a terror of repetition. Sanity sometimes seems like a very thin membrane, through which it would be all too easy to fall again. I have to remind myself that there's nothing to fear here. A harmless, if wildly improbable, coincidence. Before I can change my mind, I write a quick email to Heathcote, attaching the photo of the magpie standing proudly on my chest—exactly as Jack Daw did to him thirty years ago.

Yana returned from her job in Paris a few days ago to find the magpie and me fully enmeshed. I seem to be his tree now and he takes any opportunity he can to cling to my arm, or scurry onto one of my shoulders, or up into the nest of my hair. And even though he shits on me, and pecks at my extremities, and screams right in my ear hole, I get the sense that he's looking up to me, watching and waiting for me to show him how to be.

I'm not sure what sort of life lessons he's been learning on his journeys with me around the house. Not, I suspect, useful ones about foraging—unless my rummaging around in the fridge counts. Most of the time, he's just been perched on the edge of my desk, watching everything I do: cocking his head to one side as I sharpen a pencil and tracking the rough ribbons of wood as they fall into the wastepaper basket. Following my fingers as they drum on the keyboard and pecking at the keys too. Often, as often as he can, he steps on my wrist, or shuffles up onto the back of my hand and sinks in for a nap, a warm ball of fluff that sways and squeaks a soft reprimand if I continue attempting to type.

The parasite in his throat seems to have simply faded away and, although he celebrated Yana's return with another of his seizures, his general trajectory seems to be upward. This bird is bucking the trend.

Between feedings I've been reading around the subject as much as I can. As well as Heathcote's poem, I have been hungrily absorbing books written by people who have had encounters with this family of birds and by biologists who have studied them. The things I've discovered are astounding. Magpies are one of the few animals, other than humans, who have been shown to recognize themselves in mirrors, implying that they are self-aware. They play. Practice deception. Are masters of imitation. I read more, learning about the tiny miracle of the corvine mind; how crows and their ilk have one of the highest brain-to-body ratios in the animal kingdom; how these brains are folded densely in on themselves like Japanese steel, which allows them to punch way above their cerebral weight. *Birdbrain*, it seems, isn't such an insult after all.

I read that magpies are roughly as clever as toddlers, and that other members of the corvid family are even smarter. The New Caledonian crow, for instance, has been shown to possess reasoning powers equal to that of a seven-year-old. Striking though it is, the comparison with human intelligence seems wrong. This roving, pecking creature is not a semi-developed human stuck in a bird's body. It is an entity all its own, a totally different intelligence that is developing in front of us.

I start to get quite excited. Perhaps, I say to Yana, this will be the start of something huge: a meeting of avian and human minds, first contact. Maybe, when we release him back into the world, he'll tell the other birds about how we looked after him. I imagine being able to stretch my arms out under a tree and them hanging heavy with the weight of the wild magpies and crows who come down to greet me. Yana raises an eyebrow at this but, nevertheless, we start to interact with the bird in new ways. Does he like the things we like? Respond to the same things we respond to?

We're no longer looking at this as a simple rescue mission. We're starting to bond. Yana takes the bird on her wrist and shows him the magpie in the mirror. He stares at himself, a blue-eyed, black-beaked beauty, and emits a rolling cheep, a birdlike purr. I pick late-spring flowers from the patch out front and offer them to the creature as he rests in the folds of a towel on top of our ironing board. He takes them in his beak one after the other, tiny forget-me-nots, poppy petals twice the size of his head, and squeaks in apparent appreciation. I come home from a run to the shops to find Yana and the magpie sitting together—Yana cross-legged on the bed, the bird fluffed up on her bare shoulder, his legs invisible beneath his frilly black-and-white skirt of feathers—both listening to a piece of classical music, a haunting organ melody. Yana whistles along and the bird chirrups and peeps erratically along with her.

As the bird quests and pokes around the room, interrogating the things he comes across—my laptop charger, a cactus, a pair of sunglasses—with his increasingly powerful beak, I wonder how it is that I've come this far in life without having noticed the personhood, for want of a better word, of these animals. I realize that, if I've thought about them at all in the past, it's been as mere decorations, flashes of black and white that occasionally shoot prettily across the sky. The mental transformation feels almost magical, like walking out into your garden and finding the flowers deep in conversation with one another.

He's still unable to feed himself, or quench his own thirst, and spends great stretches sleeping, but between naps and feedings the magpie has begun to sculpt himself into shape. Having first roughly chiseled himself out of the smooth marble of his egg, he is now working on the finer details, refining the form. Where bare skin was, hard, waxy sheaths have begun to emerge; so-called pin feathers. The bird scratches and scrapes and pecks and wears them down until they crack and flake and brand-new feathers are revealed. Wherever he sits he leaves behind piles of dandruff from these feather delivery tubes. He unfurls his wings for the first time—not to flap, but to whittle away at more of these pins, the feathers coiled up tight within like scrolls. The color of these feathers, the wing feathers, is, like the bird's eyes, utterly unexpected. In the sun they shine electric blue, like the flash of the fin of an exotic aquarium fish, like no color I have ever noticed before on a native British bird.

Chapter 7

Beautiful, intelligent, and mysterious though the magpie is, Yana and I both need a break. I haven't felt clean or well rested for over a fortnight now. My eyes feel heavy and swollen from lack of sleep. There's meat juice on my shirt and bird mess matted into my hair. We're meant to be spending our spare time planning our wedding—it's coming up fast now, in a matter of months—but instead we've been playing house with a bird.

While I wash, Yana feeds the magpie to bursting, and then we go out for lunch. This is the first time we've left the creature unattended. Outside, I pay more attention to the wild birds than I ever have before. It's a huge paradigm shift to suddenly think of them as individuals, with their own unique biographies and tastes. Pigeons bob their heads to take cautious sips of oily water from the gutter, their necks flashing purple and green; a black carrion crow mounts a trash can, tossing disposable coffee cups and empty fast-food boxes to the pavement before flying off with what looks like a bag of dog shit in its beak; and an adult magpie runs along a window ledge above our heads issuing a percussive rattling cry like a burst of machine gun fire.

Heathcote hasn't replied to my email yet, although his response to our wedding invitation finally came through our letter box: a brown paper package containing a bundle of cards. From what I can tell, he seems to have responded to a simple question with a riddle. I certainly can't work out if he intends to come or not. I've been waiting for the opportunity to show Yana. Hopefully she's a better cryptologist than I am.

When we arrive at the café down the road, I empty the contents of Heathcote's parcel onto the table for her to see. She picks up the first card and reads Heathcote's message.

Charlie,

Thanks for the beautiful invitation. I'll respond in another way, if I may.

Dad xx

"I don't understand," Yana says. "What does he mean he'll respond in another way?"

She frowns and turns the card over, looking for clues. On the front of the card is a print of a surrealist painting of an owl. The owl is flying across a starlit sky with a rope in its beak. A man in stripy pajamas is inching along the rope with a butterfly net in his hands, trying to catch the owl. If he succeeds, they'll both plummet to their deaths.

"Maybe the picture is his answer?" I suggest. "Do you think he's meant to be the owl—and our wedding is the net?"

"So who're you supposed to be in all this?" Yana says. "The fat man in the ugly pajamas?"

She flips through the rest of the envelope's contents looking for clues. Along with the postcard, Heathcote has sent us a photograph of former mayor of London Ken Livingstone. Ken is holding up one of Heathcote's books of poetry and grinning. Yana scratches her head.

"I don't see what he has to do with our wedding," she says, turning to the next card, which is a print of a painting by Heathcote of a field filled with crushed Coca-Cola cans. The next is a picture of a gorilla rudely raising its middle finger with one of Heathcote's poems superimposed on top; and then, finally, a picture of Jesus, also raising his middle finger, accompanied by the same poem. The poem itself is short and not especially wedding themed. "All Anarchy Means / Is *No Bullying*! It's simple: / *Up Yours All Bullies!*"

"I'm not getting yes vibes from any of these," Yana says. "But I don't think it's a definite no either. Two kisses. I guess we'll just have to wait and see if he turns up on the day."

I don't know what I was thinking inviting Heathcote to the wedding. I knew it was a mistake at the time, seeding a dark cloud on a sunny day. I suppose part of my motivation was to make visible the gap between his version of reality and mine, and to give him the chance to close it. Is he really Dad, with two kisses? If so, he'll come.

Yana sets the pile of cards to one side. She has little patience for mind games, and there are other things to discuss: practical problems to be overcome as well as psychological ones. Her own family is pouring in from all over Europe: Her mum and dad and their respective partners, her three sisters, and her two brothers, and there's the question of where they're all going to stay. There's a grandmother in Ukraine struggling with visa issues and arthritis. We still don't have rings, or vows, or even a willing priest. All we've really settled on is the location: a riverbank on the farm where I grew up, surrounded by water lilies, weeping willows, and meadowsweet.

Long before we're on to coffee, conversation meanders back to the bird. Yana wonders when he will learn to feed himself, when he will learn to fly, and whether we can do anything to speed up the process so we can put him back into the trees where he belongs. I feel a pang at this. I'm not so sure I want him to leave, although I know he eventually must. I've grown attached. The creature is fascinating in his own right, but in addition to his inherent charm, he's become all tangled up in my head with Heathcote, his jackdaw, his never-explained disappearances, his inability to care. Part of me thinks the magpie has answers, ones he hasn't yet shared.

As Yana laps at the froth on her cappuccino, I start drumming on the table and squirming in my seat. I have an animal need to return to the nest. I've been away far too long, and the longer I stay here, the more likely it is that something untoward will happen in my absence. It's like there's a cackling alarm call going off inside my head, a mother magpie feeling. Yana spots what's going on and clings defensively to her coffee. It isn't exactly a new phenomenon, this sudden, urgent, and totally irrational need to leave places and fly home. My fight-or-flight reflex has been out of whack for a while. Only now, for the first time, it's focused on something outside me: a tiny bird in a cardboard box. I pull agonized faces at Yana until she downs her coffee and gets up, cursing me all the way home.

For once, my paranoia is vindicated. In our absence, the bird has wreaked merry havoc. Soil from a potted plant is strewn across the floor, a jar of pens and pencils has been upended, the contents of Yana's sewing box disgorged. A spool of black thread has been unwound and tracked around our bedroom, crisscrossing from one end to the other as if an enormous spider had attempted to cast an evil black web. At the very end of the line is the magpie, caught helplessly in a net of his own construction, no doubt regretting the decisions that led him to this point. The bird seems to have held his own private Maypole dance while we were away, skipping round and round a table leg with the thread clasped in his beak, unwittingly tying himself in tighter and tighter knots.

The bird looks up at us and squeaks pathetically. Yana produces a sound somewhere between a snort of laughter and a coo of sympathy and rushes over to cut him loose, making careful snips with a pair of nail scissors while the bird emits squeaky whimpers. An uncharitable part of me suspects that he has done this on purpose, to remind us how utterly helpless and dependent he is, and, perhaps, to punish us, his adoptive parents, for abandoning him. If so, then his plan has worked. Yana's eyes are shining. Clearly, she is wound up in the creature too. Freed from his bonds, the bird clambers onto the back of Yana's hand, holding her hostage as he falls into a deep and trusting sleep.

Chapter 8

In magpie society, chicks deserted by a parent don't always face ruin. Magpies have their own safety nets. In nests where, for one reason or another, the male parent has gone missing, ornithologists have observed unattached magpies stepping in to court the female and even care for her offspring as if they were his own. It's a phenomenon that sits awkwardly alongside my understanding of the selfish gene theory. Surely the male magpie should toss the chicks to the floor to cut off the competing bloodline? Instead he nurtures them. Magpies, it seems, are capable of acting outside their immediate biological interests; one might even say they are kind.

That's not quite how I saw things when I gained a new father of my own. I don't recall many details about the years that followed Heathcote's disappearance, when it was just my mum and me. What can a two-year-old remember? Chasing after the black cat that used to visit the garden of the ground-floor apartment where we lived in North London, desperate to embrace it; the color of the crockery there, deep green with swirls; the stifling smell of the upholstery in my mum's old Mini as we lurched through town, the discomfort of my car seat, the taste of bile in my mouth and then hot vomit, my mum reaching over from the driver's seat with a handful of tissues. The rare clips of home video from that period show her visibly struggling. Tired. Very thin. Recently crying. She was under more than a little strain: working as a journalist, being both mother and father to me, and reeling from the shock waves of Heathcote's breakdown. She became very ill herself, unable to get out of bed for days at a time. It was stress-induced chronic glandular fever, rather than a mental breakdown, but it was debilitating nevertheless, and frightening for both of us. In my childish way, I did what I could. She remembers waking up to find meals on the pillow next to her, or at least a toddler's idea of a meal: yogurt, old grapes, bits of cheese, and whatever else I could reach from the fridge. My nursery school teacher, a kind woman called Miss Rosalie, took to turning up at the apartment and walking me in herself. Sometimes, when my mum was unwell, she ended up buying me lunch too. I took care to avoid cracks in the sidewalk. Step on a crack, break your mother's back.

David first appears in one of these home videos: a quiet, steady presence, with closely cropped gray hair and bright blue eyes. David was, like Heathcote, older than my mum and he too already had a family: three daughters and a son from his first marriage, which had ended in divorce a few years previously. But, unlike Heathcote, he didn't try to keep them secret. Unlike Heathcote, David was solid, dependable. The opposite of flighty and elusive. He nursed my mum and cared for me as if I were his own. My memories start to come thick and fast: this new man cooking dippy eggs and soldiers for breakfast, driving me to nursery school in his car, taking me on trips to the zoo, letting me bounce on his round belly, gripping me by an arm and a leg and swinging me in circles through the air, the feeling of flying and, at the same time, of being securely held. He picked up the slack Heathcote had dropped and, with his and my mum's encouragement, I gradually began to think of him as my dad.

It was only after we left our apartment behind and moved into his large canal-side home in West London that I started to have second thoughts. The move represented a change in circumstances at least as extreme as the magpie's dive from its branch into my bedroom. This new dad was a successful musician, although I was barely aware of what that meant at the time. What I could see was that having a new dad meant I also had four new older siblings who seemed quite different in temperament from me, and who were perhaps a little disturbed after their parents' messy divorce. I liked playing on my own, or at most with that neighborhood cat—typical only-child behavior. I was for the most part a secretive and somewhat anxious child, happiest hiding on the top shelf of the wardrobe with a book, a flashlight, and the doors pulled shut behind me. They, as some siblings do, squabbled and fought and threw tantrums and hit each other on the head with the TV remote and administered Chinese burns and were understandably jealous and protective of their dad. On the day we officially moved in, one of them threw my toys out the top window of the house and, later, two of them cornered me and asked me again and again who my daddy was, prodding and pinching until I delivered the right answer: Heathcote. Heathcote was my daddy. I responded with protests of my own. I filled all of David's shoes and socks with talcum powder, decorated the stairs with blobs of shit, and later went around with a pot of green poster paint and carefully daubed David's face out of every photograph I could reach.

Children have an unnerving talent for locating sore spots and poking their fingers right in. Who was my daddy? And who, by extension, was I? When I was five, David and my mum married, and not long after that he suggested I become his son in name as well as practice. Tracking down Heathcote to see if he would agree to my being legally adopted by David proved impossible. Letters were sent to every known address but he refused to respond: Perhaps he was indifferent, or perhaps he was simply unable to cope. In the end, the legal authorities interpreted his silence as assent. I remember the exact moment of transition, when I shed one father and gained another. It was my first court appearance, although unfortunately not my last. I sat on a hard wooden bench between my mum and my soon-to-be dad, squirming and sliding around on its varnished surface. I couldn't quite see the judge over the back of the bench in front as she addressed me, asking if I was happy with what was about to happen. My mum nudged me: "Say yes, Charlie." And with a thwack of the gavel, it was done. I was stripped of the name Williams and legally reborn to the Gilmour clan. At the time I was indeed happy—although there have been moments since when shame has colored this memory. I've wondered if I should've been so ready to agree; if this wasn't my first true betrayal, my abandoning of Heathcote. A crime that made meaning of later events.

Chapter 9

The day after our aborted lunch the bird takes his very first bath. Late spring is giving way to a hot early summer, and bright afternoon sunlight irradiates the magpie's feathers as he hops up onto the rim of a shallow dish. The thin black talons at the end of his articulated toes rap against the porcelain. He peers curiously into the pool and rustles his nascent tail in what seems to be an expression of excitement or anticipation. He circles the water, leaping on twig-like legs to examine it from every possible angle. It's a while before he dips his beak into the wet, first cautiously, and then with great vigor. Water slops over the side of the bowl and his beak chinks against it like a spoon rattling in a teacup.

It takes a little longer still for him to work up the courage to leap in. I suppose birds that can't swim have to be very certain about what they're getting themselves into. When he finally takes the plunge, he stands for a moment up to his ankles, his feet magnified and distorted. He hops from leg to leg then lowers his body into the water and shakes and shakes and shakes. Water droplets cascade into the air and all over the floor. He leaps in and out of the water repeatedly, gleeful as a child dive-bombing, and then it's out and onto Yana's wrist, where he shakes again, hitting us both with a musty spray.

Yana looks down at the creature. It's a pitiful sight to behold. The bird is as bedraggled and hideous as a wet cat, and tiny, so very tiny with all his feathers dampened down. His eyes and beak are the only parts of him that haven't shrunk in the wash and they now seem freakishly outsized, like a plague doctor's mask. The bird wipes his damp cheeks on Yana's sleeve and wrings water out of his tail. Yana picks up the hair dryer, places the soggy bird on her head, and begins to fan him with a gentle blast of hot air. This doesn't seem like a creature that's going back to nature anytime soon.

As the bird dries, his former glory returns. His wing feathers spark electric blue and his newly emerged tail shimmers with iridescence, changing color from gold to purple as the sun's rays bounce off it at different angles. He shines, Yana points out, like the puddles of petrochemicals in the scrapyard where he was found.

"Maybe," she says, "we should name him after that? What about calling him Benzene?"

I've been casting around for a name for the bird for a while, but nothing seems to fit. Heathcote's jackdaw was called, quite simply, Jack Daw, a name it seemed to have arrived with. Mag Pie doesn't quite have the same ring to it. In Shakespeare, magpies appear as Maggot-Pies, but Maggot-Pie is even worse. I've been trying out the names of famous thieves for size, in honor of the magpie's best-known trait. Jean Genet. Robin. Raffles. Mister Big. I'm not sure what the convention is for naming corvids, or even if there is one, so rarely do they seem to fall into human company. The tame ravens at the Tower of London, kept there to entertain the flocks of tourists who visit, often seem to be christened rather grandly:

Thor, Huginn, Muninn, Corax, Charles. These don't seem quite right for the magpie who, for all his regal attributes, isn't as pompous an animal as all that.

Naming, of course, runs against letting go. Naming is a form of claiming. But the name Benzene, with its vaporous connotations, seems to have the idea of escape built in. Benzene. Both natural and man-made. Shining, shimmering spirit that evaporates into the air. The bird has found his name.

FLIGHT FEATHERS

Chapter 10

It's approaching June and all the other magpies, I've noticed, seem to have flown the nest. The local park is full of boisterous juveniles tumbling through the trees like sequined acrobats, chasing after parents who seem less and less inclined to respond to their begging calls. One curious young magpie even came to visit us a few days ago, scrabbling along the outside of the window frame to chatter at the bird leading a pampered and freakish life within.

Benzene shows little sign of having heard this call of the wild. We are not, I have to admit, necessarily raising this magpie in the most natural way. His life seems more akin to that of a medieval prince than to that of a bird, filled as it is with music, flowers, shiny baubles, and meat. I should probably be teaching him all sorts of survival skills in preparation for his life in the wild; although I'm not sure what skills I, a technologically dependent human being, could usefully pass on. Luckily, his instincts seem to be coming online all of their own accord. These lessons from the ancestors folded up in his genetic code have been slowly revealing themselves to us. Corvids are some of nature's greatest hoarders, always preparing for leaner times by stashing food, leaving behind little crisis larders wherever they go. They carry around mental treasure maps with hundreds—sometimes thousands—of Xs marking the spot where dinner is buried. Benzene has been showcasing this incredible ability in our bedroom with gobbets of raw meat. He can feed himself at last, and what he doesn't eat on the spot he takes and carefully tucks somewhere out of sight. Any crevice will do: the USB port of my laptop, the eyelets of Yana's work boots, the folds of a discarded sock, and dozens of other places we won't get to know about until it's far too late.

Flying is a different matter. Despite the vaporous connotations of his name, Benzene is reluctant to take to the air. He can leap great heights and distances without the aid of his wings, and that seems to be enough for him. His main objective in life, from what I can tell, is to fling himself at me or Yana and cling on for as long as we will let him, riding around the house on us as if we were sedan chairs. My visits to the kitchen are often soundtracked by excited squeals as the magpie on my head requests a piece of cheese, a taste of apple, a slice of salami. He reminds me of one of those birds that spends its days clinging to the noses of crocodiles, picking scraps from between their teeth. Except, unlike the crocodile, I'm gaining no obvious benefit from this instance of symbiosis. All I get, in fact, is a head full of partially consumed snacks as the magpie carefully stashes favored treats in my locks for later.

Thinking that a little more independence might not be such a bad thing, I take him on my hand one morning and stand over the bed. His black talons are wrapped around my index finger on either side of my knuckle, tight and thin as wire rings. I slowly begin to shake him off, lowering and raising my arm as if flapping a wing of my own. The bird clings tighter still, attaching himself as firmly to my finger as a sailor in the rigging on a violent sea. I flap a little faster and the rushing air gently ruffles the bird's feathers. This is,

I think, necessary. I recall reading somewhere, during one of my frantic bouts of research, that crows are often forced to bully their offspring into flight: placing food on branches just out of reach, or even giving them a little shove. Otherwise, I suppose the lazy chicks might happily sit in their nest forever, growing fat as foie gras geese. If I don't teach this magpie now, will that be his fate?

Benzene starts to wobble, becoming unbalanced as the hand he is used to riding around on so sedately sways like a branch in a storm. His wings remain tucked stubbornly behind his back for a few seconds more—and then they unfurl like ragged fans of patterned silk. Waves of displaced air break against my cheeks. Instinct whispers and the bird stirs up a whirlwind. He is the dark, beating heart of the storm. His talons disengage and he soars—soars for a tenth of a second before gravity reasserts itself and down he goes, a dodo-ish descent to the soft mattress below.

His early solo flights are conducted with all the grace of a chicken thrown from a barn roof. Clumsy, noisy, bottom-heavy tumbles from shelves and tabletops. But within days he begins to master up as well as down. He flies joyfully to the windowsill in our bedroom to bask in the afternoon sun and snap at bluebottles; up to the highest bookshelf in the living room to hide scraps of mince within the loose dustcovers of hardbacks; onto the rim of the bathroom sink, talons clicking on porcelain, to watch with apparent interest as I shower, brush my teeth, or pee. What is it like to have a meat-eating bird gazing intently at your penis? It is unnerving.

The bird's new flying abilities add a certain amount of tension to daily life. Nothing is now safe from his destructive curiosity; no calm moment protected from the possibility of a sudden rush of wind and the feeling of talons sinking into your scalp. Anything we might be holding he considers fair game, swooping down from his shelf-top crow's nest to dip his beak into coffee, tea, red wine, soup. He can be devious about it too, as much of a trickster as the myths and legends about magpies suggest. If I manage to frustrate one of his airborne assaults he resorts to the sneak attack, feigning total disinterest until I inevitably forget about him and his untoward intentions. The instant I leave whatever bird-unfriendly thing it is—a glass of beer, or a tumbler of whiskey—unattended, he falls like a bolt from the blue and lands beak-deep. Whenever this happens, which is often, I'm always more amazed than I am annoyed. Who knew that a bird could be capable of such duplicity?

Now that he can fly and feed himself, it should be time to start thinking seriously about when, how, and where we should release him: the junkyard he came from, our garden, my parents' farm? But the thought of life without this chaotic, inquisitive, destructive creature makes me more than a little sad. Maybe, I say to Yana when she brings the subject up, we don't need to be in such a rush. What would be the harm in keeping him around, just for a little while longer?

The bird seems quite happy to carve out his own patch of wilderness in our home. At dusk he uses his new powers to flap from my shoulder to the windowsill to the rim of the enormous pot that balances over our bed. The ficus grows sideways from the wall, its branches fixed in place by some clever mechanism Yana has contrived to make it seem as if we sleep beneath a forest canopy. The bird inches along one of its slender brown stems until he finds a comfortable spot. Settling in for the night, he fluffs up his feathers, plumping the pillow of himself, and tucks his head over his wing. There's no question of turning the lights on to read in bed; instead I read the shadows on the ceiling, seeking out one that is longer, sharper, and more solid than the others, watching the magpie as he sleeps and, who knows, perhaps even dreams.

Chapter 11

In the morning the magpie falls on me like a tick and begins bullying me out from between the sheets with his sharp beak. Directly beneath where he's been sleeping, on Yana's side of the bed, white splotches have mysteriously appeared. She takes it in stride, sponging the droppings away with a bowl of warm water while I feed and fuss over the bird. But when, that evening, he flies to roost above our bed again, and we wake at dawn having been lightly spattered with shit in our sleep again, and my only suggestion is that we start sleeping under a tarpaulin, she puts her foot down, or up, or however it is you say no to a bird.

That weekend, Yana comes back from her workshop with an enormous roll of plastic sheeting, several tree branches, and a number of concrete umbrella stands. The bird can have his temporary patch of nature, but in the spare room, not ours. This halfway house between human society and the trees feels more than a little perverse. This was once a little girl's room. There are still glittery fairy stickers around the doorframe, faded and peeling at the edges. Since we moved in, it's been a refuge for homeless friends and for Yana's scattered family. Now it's to be the residence of a bird, a scrappy little carrion eater at that.

Like the sensible parent magpies in the park, Yana is slowly pushing the young bird further and further away. I, on the other hand, am drawing him closer, tying him to me with invisible strings. As well as teaching the bird to fly away, I've been training him to fly back, using succulent morsels of meat to lure him and then whistling as he flies to my arm. It only took a few days; now, wherever I am in the house, all I have to do is click my tongue and give a bright whistle and, more often than not, the magpie will materialize.

I call him to me now, listening as he launches himself from the windowsill in our bedroom and comes swooshing over the landing and down the corridor. He hovers for a moment above my arm and the downward thrust from his wings sends ripples running through the thin plastic sheeting that covers the floor. I feel a rush of exhilaration as he drops onto my wrist, as if I were the one to have just shot through the air. My dream of being able to summon the birds down from the trees doesn't seem so farfetched anymore. Communication between man and magpie really can work in both directions.

Benzene stands on his wiry legs and looks up at me expectantly, questioningly, through eyes that are beginning to slide from baby blue to the rich licorice of a mature magpie. I set him down on one of the branches in this strange indoor forest we have created. The effect is an odd one: It's like being inside a diorama, or a Victorian taxidermy display, except that the specimen is very much alive. The magpie jumps around on his new branch, stabs at a patch of lichen, strops his iron-dark beak against the dry wood.

Outside the window, and well within the magpie's line of sight, there is a lush green corridor made up of the back gardens that divide our street from the next, a sort of green valley between the high stone ridges of the houses and blocks of apartments that enclose it. It's teeming with life: crows, magpies, feral green parakeets, fat gray squirrels, ring-necked doves, wood pigeons, robins, wrens, tits, blackbirds, goldfinches, occasionally even jays come careening through with their mad eyes and catlike screams, and red-tailed woodpeckers that do their best to compete with the percussive clatter of nearby building work, and a sparrow hawk that falls quick and deadly as lightning to snuff out the lives of songbirds that linger a heartbeat too long on the neighborhood's abundantly stocked feeders. It seems to me to be an unusually biodiverse patch of urban wilderness. Much of the land has gone quite wild. Beyond the wooden fence at the end of our small garden is a long and totally untended patch of ground, riotously overgrown with thickets of brambles and tender-stemmed elderberry bushes; and even the more carefully manicured garden plots seem like nature's honeypots. Next door the fruit on a mature cherry tree is just starting to blush and from the way the parakeets and wood pigeons are gathering I feel certain that the cherries are not destined for human lips.

A row of sycamore trees towers over it all. These enormous trees are the stages on which much of the daily drama of the urban birds is acted out and the corvids are, of course, the main players. The crows, magpies, and jays chase each other through the branches, gronking, cawing, cackling, croaking, and shrieking at one another, sometimes banding together to scream abuse at any cats who dare to venture into their realm.

At first the bird within doesn't pay much attention to all this rough and exciting action. He seems happy in his diorama, hunting flies and wolfing down strips of beef. But left alone in there, with the door closed, it doesn't take long for him to notice the disparity between his bare branches and the living, swaying, squawking world outside. I try not to get upset as he runs backward and forward along the windowsill, looking for a route through the glass. I rearrange his branches, buy him shiny new toys, release insects into the room, but none of these are quite enough.

"Don't you think," Yana finally says one day, "that it's time to let the magpie out?"

I know she's right. None of us can go on living like this. When the bird is at large in the house, fun though it is to have such a mischief-maker on the loose, I get no peace, can't hold a thought, or a conversation, without being struck by a purple flash of feathers. It's a very noisy and messy type of hat to have to wear quite so often. But shutting him away doesn't improve matters. Then he shouts and cackles and I feel as guilty and conflicted as if I'd imprisoned a mad relative in there rather than a bird. Friends are both charmed and concerned. "You have a toxic relationship with that bird," one says severely.

The magpie has been with us for a month and a half now. It can fly. It can feed itself. There's no pretending that it's ill. I know the bird has to be free, but I also know that I desperately don't want him to leave. I can't bear the thought of him disappearing forever.

These opposing urges play tug-of-war inside my head and before I even really know what I'm doing, I've taken the magpie on my wrist and am striding toward the back door.

"Come on then," I say. "Let's take him out."

With Yana following nervously behind, I open the door and step out into the garden. This is the first time the bird has been outside since he tumbled from his nest; the first time he's ever been outside with the ability to fly. The sky above us is gray and close. The air is hot and thick with the threat of a summer storm. Two black carrion crows up in the branches of one of the sycamore trees spot us and gronk censoriously at the sight of such an unusual trio. The magpie cowers, pressing himself as close to my skin as he can squeeze. I look at Yana and see tears brimming in her eyes.

"Not like that," she whispers hurriedly. "Bring him back inside."

Chapter 12

I suppose I've never been very good at letting things go. Being adopted by David did not mark the end of Heathcote. Quite the opposite, in fact. It was around the time of my adoption that he began to take on a life of his own. I might not have remembered our time in the cottage among the trees, but that didn't stop me from wondering about it. It seemed like a reality that was still running alongside me, somehow, like a train on a parallel set of tracks; and at times of loneliness, or alienation, or upset, it felt like somewhere I might belong. It was my own, private, fantasy of flight.

Most of the time, I was a cheerful enough child. I muddled along with my new siblings as best I could, and my new dad slowly and patiently won me over. The green paint was washed off the picture frames, the talcum powder shaken from his shoes, and I didn't try anything like that again—at least not for a while. One day David discovered that my older siblings couldn't tell the difference between a cabbage and a lettuce, so we began to spend weekends in the countryside, and then moved there permanently, to the farm in Sussex where my parents still live. More children followed: my two little brothers and my little sister, a small herd let loose on the farm. It was a dream childhood: full of care and affection; campfires and dogs. We landed on our feet. I should be thankful, and I am.

But there's no accounting for the perversity of the human mind. Like a tongue seeking out a sore tooth, my mind kept on probing the tiny hairline fracture running through this perfect picture. Heathcote, for all his absence, was very present: Ever since I can remember, he was always within easy reach, right there on the bottom shelf of my bookcase. It was after the adoption that I began getting him out. Alone in my room at the top of the house, before we moved out of the city, I'd take his books off my shelf and spread them out on the carpet. The whale book. The dolphin book. A single postcard tucked inside a dustcover: "*For Charlie, Love Dad*." In these moments, a strange sadness would come over me; a sense of loss and longing; a feeling of homesickness for a home I'd never really known. I felt trapped; caught on the cusp between two worlds. I have a crystal-clear memory of getting up on a chair, peering out of my window at the street below, and thinking about falling, wondering if this life would just carry on without me if I fell through it.

Who's your daddy? I wasn't sure if I really had the right to call David mine. But where was this other dad, this peculiar man who seemed to have magical powers over animals? Why had he disappeared? And would he ever come back? It was a luxury problem, really: a surfeit of fathers. My mum tried to help me make sense of the question by splitting the paternal role in two. Heathcote was my father and David was my dad. One was nature; the other nurture. She never tried to cover Heathcote's existence up and always answered my questions to the best of her ability. She clearly still admired him a great deal, despite everything he'd done. He was a genius, she said. A sad and troubled genius. She told stories about him that made him come alive, although never in front of my dad. It was like a secret between us. As to why he'd left, the answer wasn't very clear. He was a coward. He was mad. He had poetry to write. I'm not sure if my mum really knew the answer herself. She always went to great lengths to tell me what a good baby I had been, how I never cried, trying to reassure me that I hadn't been the cause, but I never quite believed her. Babies, I thought, must be terrible things, if having one is enough to turn a man mad and make him run for years without looking back.

To my childish mind, Heathcote seemed like an ideal father: a Fagin-like figure who would teach you to steal handkerchiefs and let you drink gin. A man who willfully broke the rules; who could levitate and eat fire. David, while no disciplinarian, enforced basic rules like bedtime, schooltime, homework time, no stealing, no running around on the roof, no setting fire to things, no filling water guns with urine and squirting them at visitors, no secretly marinating the Sunday roast with earthworms, no filling the fridge with wasps. I did not always obey these rules. Once when my mum admonished me for some infraction with the exhortation to "do as your father tells you," my whispered response was: "Which one?" I felt certain that in my other life with Heathcote chaos was the only decree. Not that I ever articulated these thoughts out loud. That one unheard whisper was the only occasion on which I let slip that I was living under two regimes. This divided loyalty was an invisible barrier between my dad and me: unspoken but tangible, at times literally physical. He remembers an occasion when I spontaneously hugged him because it happened so rarely.

On trips to London, I silently fantasized about running into Heathcote. I'd keep my eyes open for him, looking up into the faces of people I passed on the street with a mixture of hope and dread.

Often, I imagined I had seen him in a familiar-seeming silhouette or a bushy tangle of dark hair. The more I looked, however, the more I realized how little idea I had of whom I was looking for. I searched for Heathcote in the faces of street performers, raffish men with silver streaks in their hair, and homeless drunks begging in doorways, unsure which of these he was more likely to be.

I kept this longing to myself for as long as I could. It felt very disloyal: to my mum, who'd been so hurt, and especially to my dad, who'd raised me as his own. But then, when I was twelve, my mum gave birth to a little girl. Two blond-haired, blue-eyed brothers had preceded her, and their grating cries had, for the most part, confirmed my theories about the malevolent power of babies. But something about this baby was different. She was tender, vulnerable. The need for babies to be enveloped and protected, loved and held, was written all over her. The fact that, like me and my mum, this baby had brown hair and a button nose probably had something to do with it, too. I saw myself in her in a way I hadn't with the others. One day, watching my mum sway slowly back and forth in a rocking chair with the baby nestled on her chest, I found myself suddenly overcome with emotion. Something about this loving tableau brought all my hidden yearnings to the surface. It happened too quickly for me to go and hide, so I had to try to ride it out. My mum glanced up from the baby to see tears pouring silently down my cheeks. She was as shocked as I was. I never cried, never really let anything slip. She gently teased an explanation out of me and promised to see what she could do.

It turned out to be quite easy to see Heathcote. I'd imagined that he'd hang on to his solitude as stubbornly as a clam. But, after a mutual friend of his and my mum's got in touch, he hopped on a train to Paddington Station and we met there, at a branch of

YO! Sushi. My dad was the one to escort me. He steered me across the busy concourse toward the circular fish bar where Heathcote was waiting on a high metal stool: a scruffy-looking man in a tweed jacket with patched elbows and leather buttons. My dad stuck out his hand and Heathcote jerked oddly toward it, looking down in amusement at his own hand, which, thanks to the powerful magnet he had hidden up his sleeve, refused to budge from the metal bar top. The two of them exchanged a few neutral words and then my dad squeezed my shoulder and left.

Heathcote didn't explain where he'd been, or why we were only meeting now for the first time since I was a baby, or offer any explanation as to why he'd left—and I didn't ask. He gave the impression that the thought that I might want to see him simply hadn't occurred to him. I was childishly happy to be in his company, drinking infinite refills of green tea and watching little plates of sweaty fish pass by on the conveyor belt in front of us. I thought he looked a little like I might if I sat in a bath of vinegar for a few weeks: a goblin-like man with a pointy chin and mischievous chestnut eyes. He was brimming with magic. Not just the magnet attached to the inside of his sleeve with a piece of elastic, which he used to make tuppenny pieces disappear. His pockets, too, were stuffed full of tricks: fake thumbs, coins that could be made to melt through the palm of your hand, a spool of near-invisible spider silk thread for making objects appear to float through the air.

In retrospect, I suppose he was desperate to impress; or, perhaps, he was just desperately scared. One of the stories he told—the only one I remember, in fact—was about a vacation he'd taken to Turkey, where he'd come across a barber offering traditional hot shaves with a straight razor. Sitting with a towel draped over his shoulders and the long, straight edge of the razor to his neck, he was suddenly terrified that the suspiciously bearded barber was simply going to slit his throat and slip away with his wallet. He quickly pulled a coin from his pocket, began to perform tricks for the barber, convinced that by doing so he was charming away the man's murderous intent. At the time I thought it silly: It didn't seem likely that a barber would kill a customer in broad daylight just for a few traveler's checks. But for some reason that particular story stuck in my mind, and since then I've wondered if he was unconsciously confessing something about his approach toward me on that day: that he dreaded being made to open up, to spill, and was using magic like a matador uses his cape, to distract and misdirect, to remain untouched. Before we parted, he showed me how to perform the sleight of hand he believed had saved his life: a simple technique in which you appear to hold a coin firmly in one hand only for it to vanish into thin air.

Afterward, my mum asked me how it had gone. I thought it had gone well, although when she asked what we talked about I found that I couldn't recall very much at all, almost as if we'd talked about nothing.

I saw Heathcote again the following week. We met at the house of a magician friend of his who led us through a hidden door behind an oil painting and up a secret staircase to the roof. The three of us, peeping out from behind the chimney, breaking the rules. It felt like belonging; my *Oliver Twist* fantasy was coming true. And then Heathcote performed another of his vanishing acts. This one was of a less amusing nature. There was no warning and no explanation. One minute we were, I thought, getting along, working out a friendly relationship—he could, I'd decided, occupy an uncle-type role in my life—and then, the next, he was gone. He stopped answering my emails and the mutual friend seemed embarrassed when I asked where he was. "Well, you know Heathcote . . ." It was quietly devastating and, being a child, I blamed myself. I hadn't been interesting enough, or clever enough, or as rebellious as I needed to be to hold his attention. I drove him away. I made him disappear.

It wasn't long after this that I discovered the joy of intoxication. When I was thirteen, my older adoptive half brother gave me cannabis for the first time. It was like a thick blanket draped over the noisier parts of my mind, a warm, enveloping glow. I was instantly charmed. I discovered I had an appetite for mindlessness, and this appetite seemed to grow the more I fed it. I secretly drank stolen liquor at seven in the morning before school. Huffed fumes from a jar of gas. Pressed the heels of my hands into my carotid arteries to cut off the blood supply to my brain so I could pass out, especially at night when a light show of shameful memories kept me from sleep. Drugs, with their power to teleport you outside yourself, had an almost magical appeal.

Needless to say, I carried on paying tribute to Heathcote: stealing and pyromania and pranks. And I kept looking for him, too. I sleuthed his home address and telephone number, which I pinned on my bedroom wall and stared at for months before I dared call him. When I finally worked up the courage, I gabbled down the line, desperate to impress. He hung up and never answered my calls again, although sometimes I'd get Diana, the mother of my half sisters, China and Lily, who would coldly inform me that Heathcote was busy. The hairline fracture slid open a little wider. *I did it. My fault.* By my late teens, what had begun as youthful experimentation with drugs was beginning to look like a problem. I didn't learn my lesson. Like a bird flying repeatedly into a pane of glass, I kept on seeking Heathcote. Each time I reached out for him, the crack yawned open just a little wider, until eventually I hurtled straight through.

Chapter 13

It's not clear what fate befell Heathcote's jackdaw. His initial response to my email about the coincidence of corvids in our lives is enthusiastic enough, when it comes. He compliments the beauty of the magpie and tells me how he'd fantasized about putting his bird to work as a diamond thief. But when I try to fish for more details, he clams up, and simply refers me back to his poem. "I don't have anything else to add," he writes in response to my gentle probing. Not very dad-with-two-kisses behavior.

I've been referring to the poem often enough myself, although I can't decide whether it's a cautionary tale or a story of success. Part of me thinks that whatever Heathcote did, I should probably try to do the opposite. My bird and his are running in tandem, thirty years apart. As spring spread its wings and became summer he must have faced these same questions, and perhaps been subjected to the same conflicting urges. So what happened to the jackdaw? I pick up the now well-worn book of poems from its place on my desk. The spine is broken and there are brown splotches inside from where the magpie has tucked nuggets of mincemeat between the pages. Its lines are so familiar to me by now that I feel like I could recite it by heart. This time I look between the lines, peering through the empty space like a window into the past.

I see Heathcote as he sits on a patch of lawn just out of sight of the big house, happy as a boy in a sandbox. "There were long days of elation: digging up a patch." He sinks his trowel into the ground and grins as a section of turf comes up with a satisfying rip. The jackdaw, fixed to his head like a weather vane, suddenly comes to life and drops to the ground to examine the clod of dirt, "swooping down to display its skills as a metal detector." Jack Daw seems, in this moment, a vision of order. He struts around officiously with his wings tucked behind his back, looking over his beak at the exposed yellow roots and wormholes and bits of shale. His stiff little handlebar mustache, comprised of wiry nasal bristles, is perfectly combed, not a single hair out of alignment. He inspects the earth like an auctioneer appraising a great work of art, like a colonel reviewing his troops, like a surgeon searching for the right spot to make his first incision. He sees something, something invisible to Heathcote's mere human eyes, and plunges his beak into the muck, emerging with a tiny scrap of silver foil, which he presents with a flourish, "invoking the ghosts of picnics past." Jack Daw makes small things seem very important indeed.

Heathcote has, by now, fallen for Jack Daw's charms. Every day has been spent out here in front of the house, the bird a comforting weight on his shoulder or his head. He is Jack Daw's church tower now, he thinks, as the bird flaps back to its favorite perch. The bird has become his own personal gargoyle. Jack shrieks, a high yak-yak, *which Heathcote interprets as a demand for more. He readily acquiesces, ripping up another clod of turf for the bird to dissect.*

He feels a lightness as Jack takes off and lands in the lush grass with an elegant skip. If humans are mostly made up of water, then birds must be composed of air. Hollow bones, feathers, and wind. More of a sprite than a gargoyle, Heathcote decides.

Some hapless bug—whether an earwig, a millipede, or a woodlouse there isn't time to tell—catches Jack's attention and quick as a snake he strikes. Crunch. Ooze. Gulp. He continues with his explorations as if nothing unusual just happened. Heathcote watches as the bird brings more treasure to the surface: more foil, a bottle cap, a cigarette butt; detritus left behind by the fair that was so recently allowed to take place on the grounds; the bird an archaeologist unearthing revelries past. There is a light clack of beak on metal as Jack discovers something more substantial. A small silver coin emerges from the dark soil. Jack turns it and tests it in his beak in much the same way a pawnbroker might bite down on a gold coin to test its grade. Convinced of its value, Jack swaggers proudly over to Heathcote and stuffs it up the sleeve of his spattered suit jacket.

Heathcote leaves the coin be for a moment, watching the bird as it struts back to its pile of dirt to resume its excavation work. He remembers his boyhood fantasy, so far from the reality of life with this creature in so many ways. And yet in many ways not so far from the truth: the bird is speaking to him in a secret language, one of ruffled feathers, eye flashes, and shrieks; teaching him things nobody else can possibly know, in his own strange, violent, beautiful way; and now, Jack is bringing him treasure when he is most certainly broke.

He lets the coin slide out of his sleeve into his cupped hand. He turns it over, rubs the dirt off. A shiny silver sixpence. A miraculous thing. He passes it from one hand to the other, makes it appear and disappear, causes it to melt through his palm like liquid mercury and emerge from behind his ear, performing all his little tricks for an audience of himself and a bird.

That night, he dreams of flight: of "feathers sprouting from [his] heels" and wings bursting from his shoulder blades. He begins to suspect that Jack is dreaming of flight too. Each day when they go out he ventures a little farther from his human tower, strikes out a little more boldly in the direction of the Tamar estuary where flocks of wild rooks and jackdaws glean the mudflats. But he always returns before dusk to his perch at the foot of Heathcote's bed, from which he seems to beam his thoughts directly into Heathcote's sleeping mind.

One evening in the pub Heathcote shows off his jackdaw-mined sixpence to a visitor. "Bernie Skuse, a poacher from Bristol, said, 'Tell you what we used to do, boy. Sharpen the edge of a coin and set it under his tongue. Cut through the tendons, then he'll talk.'"

Heathcote is horrified. He doesn't want to torture the bird into speaking English. Jack is perfect just the way he is—wild, fearless, certain of exactly how to best be himself. He envies Jack this certainty, this assurance of his place in the world. It's a precious thing. He doesn't want to bend the bird to his will. He wants him to be free to follow his urges wherever they lead. And so he does: each day flying in circles that are wider and wider, farther and farther from the human sitting in the grass at the center waiting for the day to come when his bird disappears.

I place the book of poems back down on my desk. This, I reluctantly concede, isn't so far from what I'd like for the magpie. Not for him to leave, necessarily, but for him to have the freedom to choose, for him to be able to fly free and follow his instincts. Yana readily agrees. It's what she has been saying all along. But not in the back garden: too many cats, too many people around who might not appreciate a semi-wild magpie landing on their heads or invading their homes. I think about the yoga instructor next door with her ears full of jangly hoops collected on trips to India; the old geezer two houses down who likes to spend most of the afternoon smoking foul-smelling cigarettes on his doorstep; and the nearby family who barbeques steaks—Benzene's favorite—on the weekends and often leaves their delicate baby to sleep at the far end of their garden. The magpie we've raised is compatible with none of this.

"Why don't we take him with us to the farm when we go down to prepare for the wedding?" Yana says. "Let him free there?"

I think about the farm with its fields teeming with sweet grasshoppers, its centuries-old oak trees padded with soft moss, its henhouses full of fresh eggs, and its orchard dripping with plums and apples. There, the only cat for miles around is my younger sister's rotund British Blue, Norman, who is about as agile as a lump of lard that's been rolled in hair, likely to catch a bird only if it flies directly into his mouth. A magpie could get by very comfortably there: perhaps Benzene won't want to fly too far, won't be gone forever. I agree, if a little hesitantly, that the farm is the best place to release the bird; better than the scrapyard he was found in, better than here.

Chapter 14

The thought that Benzene might soon be leaving us makes our remaining time together seem golden. Yana forgives the bird for her butchered houseplants and I don't mind that Sunday has become shit-scrubbing day, because there aren't very many Sundays left. It's only a few weeks until our wedding the first weekend in August and we'll travel down to Sussex before then to start the preparations. Yana is determined that we should make everything for the wedding from scratch. Her sewing and sawing and hammering have lately reached fever pitch: tables, benches, long green cushions, and a beautifully dyed tablecloth have all been conjured into existence at her workshop. There are more things—a stage, a geodesic dome, the wedding cake, the flower displays—that have to be put together "on-site," as Yana has taken to referring to my family home. We'll take the bird, then. It makes a sort of symbolic sense: one bond is about to be formed, another perhaps broken. The wild exchanged for the domestic. It's a giddy time, teetering on the edge of this double precipice. A marriage to be made and a magpie to be lost, neither of which I could possibly have imagined just two short years ago.

The magpie, obviously, remains unaware that his fate has been tied to our wedding date. He does, however, take an active part in the preparations, sticking his beak into Yana's sewing machine and treating the procession of visitors who arrive bearing swathes of fabric and shiny baubles as if they had come to pay tribute to him. Human society seems to be just as interesting to Benzene as his natural society in the trees.

The most popular visitor by far is Rupert, a jewelry dealer friend who comes around one particularly sunny afternoon dragging a battered suitcase full of precious metals and stones behind him. Benzene gazes at him, transfixed, as we perch on the sofa to pick something out for the wedding. To Benzene's delight, Rupert tinkles and glimmers whenever he moves. Every single body part is draped in as much swag as it can carry: thick gold and silver chains jostle for position on his neck and wrists, each finger holds as many rings as will fit, diamonds sparkle from the lobes of his ears, and a silver pin dances on his tongue whenever he speaks. Benzene climbs slowly onto the back of Rupert's hand, apparently hypnotized. The complex blues of his wing feathers and the green-gold flash of his tail far outshine anything Rupert pulls from his case. Nothing, not even diamonds, can compete. It makes our job of choosing something very hard.

Benzene slowly emerges from his trance. He fixes his beak around an enormous purple stone that sits on a ring on one of Rupert's fingers and tugs. It strikes me that, rather than being hypnotized, he was simply frozen with indecision.

"No, darling, you can't have that," Rupert says. "That's Byzantine silver, worth more than your nest."

Benzene moves on, working his way from one finger to the next, checking for loose fixings, weak links. What is fascinating about this behavior is that it is pure myth. Magpies have a reputation as hoarders of shiny objects. But this has been shown to be nonsense. A study conducted at the University of Exeter a few years ago proved as much. In fact, the scientists discovered that magpies often acted fearfully around novel shiny objects and very rarely even picked them up.

So, what is Benzene doing working his way so determinedly up Rupert's arm toward the diamond that rests like a dewdrop on the soft flesh of his ear? Brought up by humans he is somehow reflecting the human idea of what a magpie should be. Either that or he is able to read our desires: hence his appetite for cigarettes, five-pound notes, and bike lock keys, as well as priceless jewels.

Rupert grins as the magpie tugs on the bits of metal that hang from various parts of his face. I suspect most passing strangers in this densely populated city wouldn't take it so well. If he is to fly free, the farm is definitely where he must go.

Rupert yelps as the bird pulls a little too hard on his nose piercing and quickly offers him a trinket, a cheap alloy ring with a skull motif. We've all been so distracted by the magpie's escapades that he is somehow the only one to emerge from this encounter with a ring. He turns it over in his beak, *click-clack*, and flies up to his crow's nest where, contrary as ever, he is amassing a collection of small shiny things.

chapter 15

How fast can the average magpie travel? Twenty miles per hour? Thirty? Not, certainly, as fast as Benzene, who is whizzing effortlessly along at sixty miles per hour, now seventy, as I drift into the fast lane to overtake a truck. I'm driving my mum's old car, an avocado-green Fiat Multipla, to the farm. It's an eccentric vehicle in many ways. I like to think that it brings joy wherever it goes but I suspect that people are generally laughing at, rather than with, its bulbous exterior and garish color scheme. But with three seats in the front as well as the back, it was good for the school run, and it's good now, on this interspecies family run. No magpie at least has ever journeyed in such style.

Benzene sits in a travel cage, strapped into the extra seat between Yana and me, staring brightly ahead as the road and sky rush past in a blur. He has never seen sights quite as amazing as those we pass on the way to the farm: electricity pylons, rolling fields, sheep, cows, Croydon. Occasionally I take one of my hands off the wheel and slide a live mealworm between the bars, listening as he cheeps happily and crunches it down.

Corvids line our route like spectators at a parade, watching as we pass. Wild magpies stand on the hard shoulder in their undertaker tails waiting to carry away trash and roadkill; rooks strut around the service station like Venetian noblemen in black pantaloons, stabbing at discarded fries with their rapier beaks; a carrion crow perches on top of a speed camera praying for collisions. Now that my eyes have been opened to the omnipresence of the corvid family by the magpie strapped in beside me, I realize that wherever you go, crows are watching, making note of our habits, our weaknesses, our wasteful tendencies. This watching has enabled them to adapt to the most powerful and destructive ecological force on the planet: us. And not just to survive—to prosper.

This intelligence, this incredible ability to read another species, has made us late, very late. I've heard of the Devil's Hour—the extra sixty minutes it takes for parents of young children to make it out the door—but magpie hour must be a new one. Somehow, despite having never been caged in his life, the magpie seemed to know exactly what he was in for when I emerged from the basement with an old cat carrier in hand. Eventually I managed to coax him down from the ceiling with a piece of costume jewelry. Benzene's interest in all things humans value can, it turns out, be used against him, although the diamanté tiara was little consolation when I closed the cage door behind him.

Despite having known this bright, inquisitive, mischievous creature for a couple of months now, I puzzle over how such a tiny brain, contained within a skull no larger than a walnut, could possibly have room for such an imagination. Perhaps the bird is capable of reading intention as well as desire. Or perhaps he simply has an instinctive fear of the new. I still don't know how much to credit the complexity of the magpie mind.

Benzene is becoming unsettled again. He jumps onto the side of the cage and squeals pleadingly. The sight of his articulated talons wrapped like fingers around the bars is more than I can bear. Keeping the car steady, I pull a cover over the cage and plunge the bird into pacifying darkness.

Heathcote hovers like a cloud over the journey. Just before we left, I sent him another email. His old school friend Peregrine Eliot has died. I commiserate, ask Heathcote if he's okay, tell him I understand if he doesn't feel up to a wedding. But I bargain with him a little too: There's the ceremony at the registry office in Brighton the next day. He could jump on a train and show his face. "Just for the sake of a complete picture," I write. "No pressure." Bird. Windowpane.

As we veer off the main road, I wind down the windows and take the cover off the magpie's cage so he can get his first look at what might very well become his new home. Wood pigeons weigh down the branches of the cherry trees that line the drive. A pheasant cock rattles his feathers of polished bronze in the long grass. A woodpecker, green on green, shoots on a sine wave toward the tree line. The magpie doesn't miss a thing.

The car's tires crunch over the gravel beside the house and Yana and I step out and stretch. The air is thick with the smell of the rosemary bushes that grow against a low brick wall, the lavender beds that buzz and hum, and the silky red roses whose heads loll sleepily from a vine that grows up the side of a whitewashed outbuilding.

My mum is already striding toward us with a sandy-haired mutt at her heels. People sometimes mistake us for siblings, to her eternal delight. She has brown hair and brown eyes, like mine, but her skin is a couple of shades darker. She embraces us both and then peers into the car.

"Let me see him properly, then," she says. "My first grandson."

I'm not sure how I feel about this. Ever since Yana and I announced our wedding plans I've noticed a certain sort of pressure building. Every visit to the farm now seems to involve compulsory viewing of baby-photo albums. I keep getting handed actual babies whenever there's one to spare and told how well it suits me. And when Misha, Yana's dad, arrived from Sweden, I heard him raising a secret toast in his gravelly voice: "To babies."

Magpies have their own womb-worrying powers, too: see three at once and a girl's on the way, four for a boy. One magpie, I remind my mum, is for sorrow.

"Not this one," she says with infuriating certainty. "His room awaits."

We install Benzene in a small bedroom halfway up the stairs. At my behest, we're waiting until after the wedding to release him. Letting go—not my forte. In anticipation of the magpie's arrival, the room has been thoughtfully covered in tarpaulins—and filled with baby toys.

"We thought he'd like something to do while you're busy getting married," my mum says with a mischievous glint in her eyes, tugging a string attached to a plastic duck and waving it at the magpie as it quacks out "The Blue Danube."

That done, we sit around the kitchen table going over the guest list and discussing who else will need rooms in the house. A friend of Yana's who is giving birth a week before the wedding probably shouldn't be made to sleep in a tent. Nor should my truly ancient great-aunt.

"What about Heathcote?" my mum asks.

I've shown her his cryptic RSVP. We puzzled for a while over the meaning of the man in the pajamas chasing the owl and both found it as frustrating and fruitless as trying to interpret someone else's dream. But there's something else, something I've been holding back.

"I did promise him a bed in the house," I say. "But I'm not sure if he'll be filling it."

I promised him a car to ferry him to and from the riverbank as well as anything else he might need to make things easier. This was the last time I saw him face-to-face, this past winter before the magpie arrived, at one of his crusty poetry events in London. I hadn't been invited, I'd just heard he was going to be there and turned up. I was shocked by how poor his health was. He needed help getting up the stairs to the event space and once there had to sit wheezing on a sofa for half an hour to recover. Perhaps it wasn't the right moment to spring an introduction to my fiancée and an invitation to our wedding on him—but if not then, then when? I told him about the riverbank, about how beautiful it is in summer, about how an anarchist professor he greatly admired was coming along too. I didn't mention it, but I had especially invited this professor so that Heathcote would have a friend. He could just drop in for an hour or two if he wanted.

"Why," Heathcote had hissed, "would I want to come to a wedding on some rock star's farm?"

"Well," my mum says, striking his name off the list, "we won't reserve a room for him then, and if he does turn up he can just sleep in a bloody ditch."

My dad, sitting inconspicuously in an armchair in the corner, shakes his head, part amused, part outraged. He is roughly the same age as Heathcote and cast in a similar mold: another post-war baby sent straight from his mother's breast to boarding school where discipline took the place of love. No doubt they carry a few of the same emotional scars but all similarities end there. In my life at least, David has been the total opposite of Heathcote:

capable, dependable, present. A quiet, unassuming man who expresses himself, yes, through music, but more often than that through caring actions. I haven't always paid him back in kind. At times it can't have been easy for him having to compete with the fantasy father who lived in my head. How could an ass-scratching, nose-picking, school run–driving, remote control–hogging, dinner-making mortal ever compete with the genius-wizard-poet of my imagination? Only by reliably being there when the other was not. Even now, I suspect him of being secretly pleased whenever the real Heathcote acts like a total shit.

"What," he says, "a wanker."

And it's true—Heathcote is a wanker and a shit, but I'd still like it if he came.

We haven't been sitting for long when an angry rattling noise fills the air. Benzene has exhausted the possibilities of his musical duck and is now singing a special song of his own.

"He's bored in there, poor bird," I say. "Shall I go and get him?"

My younger sister herds her enormously fat cat into another room and my grandmother folds her newspaper into a bird-sized flyswatter. In China, magpies are venerated. The Magpie Festival is the Chinese equivalent of our Valentine's Day, although that particular part of my grandmother's Shanghai upbringing—unlike her habit of spitting bones onto the table and cursing the Japanese—doesn't seem to have made a mark.

Blissfully ignorant of all this, Benzene surfs into the kitchen on the back of my hand, tilting his head rapidly in all directions. Birds cannot move their eyes independently of their heads like we can, so they have to crane their necks at anything they want to see. Benzene bobs with curiosity.

Having scanned the room to his satisfaction, he hops from my hand to the table and proceeds to make his introductions. He bows, he flutters, he squeaks. He strides along the tabletop as if it were the most natural thing in the world. Tosses a few peas off my plate. Has a stab at the gem on my mother's wedding ring. Swills my dad's lukewarm tea around in his beak. Everyone is very gung ho about this. Just another eccentric guest.

The mutt, Doris, studiously ignores the bird, which makes me suspect—from the way she has ignored roast chickens, pies, and birthday cakes in the past—that she is giving serious thought to eating him on the sly. He peers down at her over the edge of the table and she avoids making eye contact, as if worried about having her mind read. My mother tuts at her and slips a muzzle over her snout.

The bird reaches the far end of the table where my grandmother stabs at her food with a slightly sour expression on her face. No muzzling her. Benzene quacks and bows, and as he does so his tail swishes through the air like a conductor's rod.

"Hello, you horrible thing!" my grandmother says.

Benzene hears this as an invitation and steps onto her wrist. He tests the sponginess of her flannel shirt with his talons then sinks his head into its folds. The bird squeals with some sort of unfathomable delight. The corners of my grandmother's mouth twitch and then she breaks into an unwilling grin. Benzene isn't like "those other magpies," she declares.

It doesn't take much: a flash of gold here, a burst of mischief there, and before long Benzene, the clever little crow, has embedded himself in this new and luxurious nest as seamlessly as a cuckoo. Once the wedding is done, we'll let him fly free, but for now at least, he's one of the family.

Chapter 16

The day of the wedding begins much like any other. The magpie shouts me out of bed around sunrise. I tiptoe hurriedly down the corridor as he screams for his breakfast, hoping that I'm the only one in the now very full house who has been woken by his horrible crowing. I fill his worm bowl, slice up some slivers of beef, roughly scramble an egg, throw in a crust of bread, a grape, a piece of carrot. Then I sit with him awhile in the dust-mote dawn. The sun is just trickling through the branches of the old oak that grows by the house. Tiny songbirds whistle and chatter as they tease their breakfasts out of its fissured bark. A carrion crow high in the canopy croaks five times. The magpie sucks a worm down his gullet headfirst.

I chat to him unselfconsciously as he eats, telling him about the wedding, how it unfortunately means that he'll have to stay locked away for most of the day, but how that's okay because he'll be soaring over the roof and through the trees soon enough.

Benzene flaps onto my head and I feel his beak rattling against my scalp as he hides a few choice morsels of meat in my hair. I don't know why he does this. It can't be for safekeeping because he very rarely returns to reclaim food hidden in this way. I like to think he is presenting me with small tokens of his appreciation but his fury if he catches me removing such treasures suggests otherwise. I shake my head over the tarpaulin and watch as, with squeals of outrage, Benzene scuttles around gathering the fallen meat back up again.

I back out of the room and shut the door. Today is not about the magpie and there is still much to be done. Yana has a cake to finish making, bridesmaids to dress and prep, headdresses to stitch and glue. I have the magpie's last few meals to comb out of my hair and a best man to drill. Three of Yana's sisters arrive after breakfast in a van laden with flowers. We set up a production line at a long table in the old stable yard, turning out bouquets and flower crowns in the rising heat.

In the kitchen, Yana ices the cake with one hand and wields a glue gun with the other. Guests start to arrive, and my younger brothers direct them to the river. Rupert, the magpie's favorite jewelry dealer, comes with a pair of sharp goldsmith's pliers to fix tiny rubies to the gold chains we chose instead of rings. The anarchist professor bustles into the house, flapping his arms about something or other, and has to be shooed away from the half-made canapés.

With minutes to go before the ceremony, Yana slips off to change. She returns looking beautiful and strange. The dark silk of her dress is patterned like the dusky corner of a painting by Hieronymus Bosch. Things leer out of the shadows: From her ankles all the way to her neckline coral-red snakes vie for space with fleshy summer flowers. A memento mori looms pale as a moon from her side. Real dragonflies sparkle in her hair. As we walk out onto the sunlit path that leads to the river, flecks of gold light up in her olive-green eyes.

A clattering of jackdaws bursts into the air as we pass by their field. Two magpies ride helter-skelter through the branches of a horse chestnut. A crow dips its wings. Heat rises in waves from the path, blurring the air, and, for one frightening instant, everything suddenly feels very unreal. The bridesmaids following behind us and the crowd of friends and family craning their necks in front of us all become as insubstantial as smoke. The world seems as flimsy as a curtain that's about to be drawn—and when it is I'll find myself alone in this field. I close my eyes, grip Yana's hand, and when I open them again the world has solidified.

Down by the river we stand on a gently sloping bank curtained by weeping willows. The dark water to one side of us, the sun-dazed guests perched on unsteady benches to the other, the ground reassuringly firm beneath my feet. My younger sister acts as priest, blessing us as we exchange chains and vows. Having shed our clothes, we plunge into the river with arms linked and everyone except for my aged aunt follows. The water slips over our skin as we soar along with the current. Thin green tendrils reach up from the riverbed to tickle our bellies. Lily pads bobble and reed beds sway. Flushes of duckweed give way as easily as clouds. Yana turns onto her back and looks up at the sky and I do the same; as close to flying as I've ever come.

As we reclothe and sit down to eat—skin singing and heads on fire—I notice the empty place for the first time. The anarchist professor doesn't seem to mind having the extra elbow room. I watch him for a moment as he piles his plate high with shrimp and delivers, between mouthfuls of flame-grilled crustacean, a lecture to his neighbor on the need to end capitalism.

Speeches soon begin. Yana's father alternates between Swedish, Russian, and English to tell a complicated story about Yana scaring all the other children at school; Yana's mother talks about how raising Yana and her two younger sisters was like living with a three-headed dragon; my widowed grandmother makes everyone cry; my mum pulls it all together with a joke. Later my dad strums an old love song. These, I think, are the only people I need around me.

But the next day, at the registry office in Brighton, I find myself looking again for the one person who isn't there. Heathcote doesn't show; not a shadow, not a whisper. I suppose I always knew that would be the case and feel stupid for having allowed myself to hope otherwise. As we drive slowly along the seafront, waving goodbye to everyone from the windows of the car, I try to put it from my mind for good. At least now I've reminded myself what Heathcote isn't—as if I needed to. The real "dad with two kisses" is grinning and waving at us from the sidewalk. Heathcote is something else.

We arrive in the New Forest—"new" when it was named by William the Conqueror a thousand years ago—sometime after sundown, winding into the ancient woodland on a narrow, unmarked lane. Dozens of ponies sleep by the road; some of them even sleep on the road, dozing on their feet in the middle of the worn tarmac with their eyes wide open. The grays gleam like ghosts in the headlights. Trees flash before us. Bent old yews shake their claws. Black poplars and thriving American redwoods shoot up like temple columns. A covert of rhododendrons swallows us whole.

The next day we walk into the woodland, a great living breathing mass. Resin drips indecently from the clefts of evergreens. Bark bursts at the seams with centuries of life. We follow a deer track into a thicket of waist-high ferns, wading through the waves of green until we find ourselves in a clearing of sweetly scented chamomile. Our footsteps bruise aroma from the wispy leaves. The low, earthy smell of the forest, the heady rush of the chamomile, the deep richness of sun-warmed skin. It's almost too much.

I can see that Yana is drunk from it too. She idly tears the petals from a chamomile flower and begins to talk about the origins of the honeymoon, why traditionally it would be one lunar cycle long. The complacent smile on my face freezes and then I begin to frown.

"What is it?" Yana says. "Do you really not want to have kids?"

I close my eyes. I'm not one for difficult conversations and this feels like it's going to be very difficult indeed. If, for Yana, children follow love and marriage as naturally as one season follows the other, then something has become stuck in me. When I try to think about having children, all I manage to summon up is a wordless ball of terror. I switch off and listen to the sounds of the forest instead. A wood pigeon whistles. A branch creaks. Somewhere far off a child screams. The silence between us hisses like static. I peep out from behind my eyelids and find Yana staring at me a little apprehensively.

Try as I might, I can't put my feelings into words. It's as if a winged creature has swooped down and snatched out my tongue. I scrabble around for excuses and diversions instead, but Yana has a quick answer to them all.

"We're so happy as we are," I say. "Why risk changing that?"

"Why," Yana says, "shouldn't we take a risk to share that happiness with someone else?"

"But won't it scream and shit and . . ."

Yana raises an eyebrow: "Magpie."

I fall silent again. As I rub my temples, Yana pulls a spoon from her back pocket and begins stabbing a circle in the turf of the clearing we're lounging in. She prizes a palm-sized plug of chamomile plants from the earth like someone shucking an oyster. From her other pocket she pulls a hotel shower cap and carefully packages up her stolen patch of nature to plant in our garden back home. She's come prepared. I think about how much of her life is about creation, about generation. She has a certainty about herself and the world that I lack.

"I still feel like a child," I begin, and then trail off, wondering what on earth I mean. I'm not a child, I'm a twenty-seven-year-old man, married even. What I mean is that I don't trust myself. I don't feel responsible. I've taken spectacularly poor care of my own person, so how could I take care of a child? What if there is a gene for abandoning babies? What if sudden bouts of insanity run in the blood? What if I repeat Heathcote's mistakes? What if I repeat my own? I don't say any of this, of course. I can barely even articulate these things to myself, can barely even hear myself think above the hissing static that is coming not from anything between Yana and me, but from within me, from this white-hot egg of fear I've stumbled across. The panic must register on my face, because Yana takes my hand.

"It's okay," she says gently. "There's nothing to be scared of."

I think about the story her dad told at the wedding about her leading the way through a forest at night when she was a little girl. The other children clung to each other, but Yana strode ahead alone into the pitch black without a flashlight, guided only by a powerful internal instrument that didn't seem to register fear. That is undeniably who she is, but it's not who I am. I shake my head and hide behind silence.

Chapter 17

The doors are open. The bird is on my wrist. We've come back from our short honeymoon to perform the wedding's inversion: the breaking of a bond. The bird and I step over the threshold. There's nothing but air between him and the horizon. Infinite possibility extends in all directions. The magpie flattens his feathers against his body, shrinking away from it all. His talons tighten their grip on my flesh. This is not what I expected. I thought he might go off like a pigeon from a box. Up and away and instantly anonymous. Who can tell one bird of the same species from another? Instead of that, I find myself having to coax him into the air.

I point out the long horse paddock, the lake, the woodland beyond, and slowly Benzene unwinds. He shakes himself like a wet dog and his feathers puff out. The tension leaves his talons. His dark eyes drink the landscape in. To me it is as familiar and comforting as the face of an old and trusted friend. I feel as if I know every tree from trunk to tip, each hedgerow inside and out. I see it in a different way now from how I saw it as a child, and in a different way again through the eyes of a bird.

Halfway down the lawn, Yana stands with her arm held in the

air. She whistles. The bird, seeing a safe halfway point between here and the horizon, throws himself into the air. His first flight out in the open since he fell from his nest. I watch in awe as he flies low over the lawn, shimmering waves of purple, blue, and green rolling from his nape to his tail. He lands, falcon-like, on Yana's outstretched wrist and then spins around to face me.

For the first few minutes this is all he seems to want to do: short, low flights from one human to another, only gradually growing in confidence as he hops from Yana, to me, to my mum, my dad, and my younger brothers.

His circles grow wider. He soars higher. I feel as if I'm being pulled along with him, like an anchor being dragged along the seafloor. This could very well be goodbye. I know that it should be. But I secretly, selfishly, hope that he'll never leave. The bird has been with us for only three months, and yet I find it hard to imagine life without him.

I whistle and back he flies, more boomerang than bird. I look at him in wonder as he nuzzles the back of my hand with his downy cheek. There are so many other things calling to him. Other magpies cackle invitingly in the distance, house martins shout insults from the gables, bees buzz temptingly around the lavender. Although I spent some time in London encouraging him to respond to my calls, with all this competing chatter it seems wildly improbable that he would actually listen. I thought he'd be lost as surely as a helium balloon that slips from your grasp. It just doesn't seem possible that a bird—truly free in nature for the first time in its life—could be so content with human company.

It could just be that he is overwhelmed by it all, that the shock of the new keeps him clinging to the familiar. All of this is strange to him. Grass comes as a surprise. He touches down on the lawn for less than a second before taking off in alarm at the unexpected sensation. It's weird and wet and seems to want to swallow him whole. In a rose bed he discovers his first earthworm. It gets lightly nibbled and then spat out in disgust. Flowers, by contrast, are a continuing source of delight. He runs from my shoulder along the length of my arm to get at a rose, which he tears to bits. Somehow, without even being told, he seems to know what he's doing is naughty and leaps skyward with a beak full of petals.

If I close my eyes, I can almost feel the wind rushing through his feathers. His weightless ecstasy is, for a moment, my own. I feel the push and pull more keenly than ever. I want him to fly away. I want him to stay.

When I look up, the bird has settled on one of the lower branches of the greengage tree that grows halfway up the lawn. As a child I used to sit on the exact same branch, whiling away summer afternoons with a Walkman for what felt like hours at a time. This time of year, it's a perilous perch. The ripe fruit attracts wasps, which burrow inside and hollow them out, swarming stickily over each other. Once, while happily daydreaming, I failed to notice half a dozen of them working their way between my toes, looking down too late to see them thirstily lapping up my sweat, powerless to move until they were done.

The magpie takes a snap at one. I whistle. He looks up at me and then quickly looks guiltily away, climbing the tree with short jumps until he's at the farthest branch, swaying like a black pennant in the breeze. I whistle again and hold out my arm, patting it encouragingly. At last, he launches himself toward me—then veers away right at the last second, rushing past in a blur of black and white. I spin around just in time to see him as he shoots up past the oak tree, over the roof of the house, and out of sight. For a moment, he disappears. I knew this was a risk. It was a desired outcome, even. I feel a mixture of sadness and satisfaction to think that he's gone, although it's quickly replaced by guilty relief. Trickster of the ages, the magpie peeks out from behind a chimney stack. He hasn't discovered his freedom, just a new game: hide-and-seek. He clicks his tongue twice in a self-satisfied sort of way and finally flies down to settle on my outstretched arm.

Chapter 18

The magpie keeps vanishing and reappearing, vanishing and reappearing. Each time he does I get the sense that time is folding in on itself. Two men. Two crows. Two losses. As I tramp through the fields after Benzene, I see Heathcote tramping alongside me in search of his jackdaw. I don't know how Heathcote felt when Jack disappeared. His writing, so clear and precise for so much of the poem, becomes elusive and obscure, like he's trying to hide something, or hide *from* something. This much I know. A day came when Jack never returned. He flew off one summer morning and that was the last Heathcote ever saw of him—or so he writes.

> *Heathcote, his shoulder empty of a bird for the first time in weeks, spends days scanning the sky and combing the trees for a hint of Jack. Any black speck draws him like a magnet. He asks everyone he meets on these meandering walks through the valley the same absurd question—have you seen a jackdaw? "Pinch something of yours?" the response comes. "That's what they do." And he realizes that, in a way, the jackdaw has. Trying to fill the bird-shaped hole*

in his life, he immerses himself in the shriek and clatter of jackdaw gatherings. "The jackdaw tribe's peripatetic parliaments. Spread across the fields, seething carpets of glistening flecks." He shows his face to each jackdaw in turn, "hoping to jog one avian memory." But it's hopeless; Jack is gone.

A tactless friend points out that, by taming the bird, Heathcote might have signed its death warrant. "You've put its life in peril. I heard of someone took a bird in, then, when they released it, it was so tame it landed on the barrel of a sportsman's gun. Got itself blown to bits, didn't it?" Never mind, the friend says, "Just a bird, wasn't it?" Heathcote becomes troubled and then, like another kind of bird entirely, he sticks his head in the sand. He retreats into myth, spins riddles, collects jackdaw facts—and the picture blurs.

How did Heathcote react? He became troubled—that's as deep into his emotional life as the poem goes. After that, his writing loses clarity, loses meaning even for a few stanzas. "Jackdaws love my big sphinx of quartz," he writes, frustratingly. A glitzy flash of nonsense to distract from the truth.

Part of me suspects he would have been glad to be free from the responsibility. But then I wonder if Jack wasn't one of the only things tethering him to some sort of reality, one of the only things reassuring him that he was a good man. He writes about the jackdaw's easy confidence, its assurance of its place in the universe, with something close to envy, and toward the end of the poem he quotes Kafka: "We find relations with animals easier than with men. Animals are closer to us than human beings." These seem, to me, like the sentiments of a lonely and lost man. It's strange, and perversely gratifying, to think of Heathcote upset at being abandoned—but then what did he learn from it?

Heathcote's tactless friend was, I suspect, right. Port Eliot—an aristocratic shooting estate—was no place for a bird that knows no fear. My mum remembers the horror of being woken up one morning by the blast of shotguns outside our bedroom window, pheasants thudding dead onto the forest floor. Perhaps Heathcote did wrong. If so, then my first instincts were correct. Whatever he did, I should try to do the opposite, although the implications of this conclusion are hard to accept.

Like jackdaws, magpies are legally considered "pests," meaning they can be exterminated with relative impunity. The farm is no shooting estate. It's practically a nature reserve. But even here the coast is not totally clear.

"The bird might be better off staying with you for a while longer," says the farm manager when he stops by one day for a cup of tea. He was, he says, on the neighboring farm not long ago. They're raising poultry and game and are catching magpies en masse with something called a Larsen trap.

Larsen traps are terrible things. A juvenile magpie—like the one happily hunting flies in the kitchen around us—is placed in the center of a cage, where it acts as live bait, a "Judas bird" that attracts others into the trap. Needless to say, it's a cruel technique, with birds sometimes being left to starve to death.

Even so, I continue flying the bird. The chances of him leaving the farm, and of then falling into one of these traps, seems remote. And a life in the trees is worth the risk.

So, over the days that follow we keep on trying to set him free. On several mornings, I wake at dawn and take him out into the fields, following the cackles of the wild magpies. We walk down the same track that leads to the river—drier and dustier thanks to the hot days since the wedding—and I imagine there is a magpie mate waiting for him somewhere around the bend. Benzene enjoys these excursions. He flies up into new trees, picks spiders from the gables of old barns, and wants to play fetch with tiny sticks. But he rarely ventures out of sight and when I turn to walk back toward the farmhouse he always follows close behind.

The local wildlife seems drawn to this freak of nature. Birds seem to come closer to the house than they ever have before: A pair of green woodpeckers settle regularly in the greengage tree; a raptor of some kind—perhaps a sparrow hawk—thuds down heavily on the garden gate while we are having lunch outside and surveys us coldly with a killer's eye; and a parliament of crows adjourns in the paddock to raucously debate the magpie situation. Wild magpies perch on the rough wooden fence that separates the garden from the horse paddock and watch Benzene's escapades. He hops around the lawn, indifferent to his avian audience, more interested in sneaking up behind humans and pulling at their socks until they chase him around or bullying the mutt into cowering submission.

The magpie situation is something we humans discuss too. Time is ticking. We have to go back to London soon and, as much as everyone here seems to enjoy Benzene's company, we can't just leave him to fill the piano with raw meat and tear the petals off all the roses.

Then one morning, as we walk together down the dusty path toward the river, Benzene answers the question for us. He suddenly takes flight. It catches me by surprise and I lose sight of him. This is a familiar occurrence by now, and I know from experience that he must be somewhere close by, lurking on a barn roof or sitting still and silent in the dark shadows of a tree.

That's where I eventually spot him, peering down at me from high up in an ash fifty meters or so away. I tramp toward him, whistling and patting my arm, but as soon as I get close, he takes off, soaring from tree to tree, ever farther. He draws me off the path and in the direction, I realize with alarm, of the alleged magpie killer's farm. I struggle over ditches, through tall grass and brambles, cutting up the insides of my legs. Soon, he abandons the trees and starts flying straight for the danger fields. I run but it's too late. This time he's really gone.

I trudge back to the house. I'm sweaty, grimy, a little bloody, and close to tears. A vision enters my head: a cage full of shrieking magpies being lowered into a watery trough, bubbling and thrashing until they're all dead, a matted mass of wet feathers and wide-open beaks.

A familiar squawk greets me as I push open the garden gate. Benzene is up on the roof, tearing off clods of moss and tossing them in the gutter. Another trick. His ability to throw holograms. Every magpie is Benzene and I'd chased the wrong one through the trees. I make my way to the front of the house, shimmy up onto a wall, and clamber carefully to join him by the chimney. The terra-cotta tiles and lead trimmings are warm to the touch—and so are the magpie's feet when he jumps onto my arm. He rubs his head against my knuckles—a sign of affection, I think. The Sussex countryside stretches out in front of us. There's nothing but air between him and the horizon. But here he is, with me.

Chapter 19

Heathcote has sent another puzzle. It's waiting for us in the hallway when we get home, in a brown paper parcel marked with his unmistakable copperplate hand. Inside I find two carefully bubble-wrapped objects. I open the smaller of the two first and snort when I see what it is, blackly amused and horrified at the same time. Sitting in my palm is a scale replica of the Cenotaph, Britain's most sacred war memorial, complete with ceramic Union Flag hanging from the side and THE GLORIOUS DEAD inscribed on the front. The real-life Cenotaph stands on Whitehall, just up the road from the Houses of Parliament, a somber tower of gray stone between the lines of traffic. The word *cenotaph* means "empty tomb," and this one stands in honor of those who lost their lives in the First and Second World Wars, although it has come to represent far more than that to many. Today it is the epicenter of an elaborate culture of remembrance. A sort of secular god to which politicians make annual televised offerings. It's an odd sort of a wedding present, to say the least. I can't see what joy it's supposed to bring Yana, a Ukrainian-Swede who visibly bristles if I dare to even so much as hum the opening bars of the national anthem. As for me, it feels like a message as well as a sick sort of joke. Heathcote must be trying, obliquely, to tell me something, although it's hard to say exactly what. Perhaps, I think, he wants to remind me of what happened the last time I tried to make him part of my life, seven years previously.

With the Cenotaph in hand, I turn back the clock. Twenty again. Driving through the streets of Jericho, in Oxford. The piece of paper with Heathcote's address, stuck to the pin board in my bedroom for so many years, is now blu-tacked to the dashboard of the car. I haven't stopped looking for Heathcote since our last encounter. I've wasted a lot of time looking for him in the places he isn't. On the Internet. On the other end of the phone line. In the dusty book stacks of my university library. There I found his plays, but no trace of him. On vacation for the summer, I've finally decided to go looking for him in the place where he is, following that now very worn little piece of paper right to his front door.

I cruise slowly down the street. To my right, a row of garages with matte black doors. To my left, the house I know to be Heathcote's. He must be somewhere behind that grimy ground-floor window, almost within reach. Something about this thought affects me deeply; the fact of his easy presence and proximity coming into conflict with my own experience of his inaccessibility. The road blurs and wobbles as hot tears flood down my cheeks. I try to wind them back in but it's no use. A dam whose existence I'd practically forgotten has burst wide open.

I'm not even really sure why I'm crying. I don't understand how this still has power over me. How can nothing, an absence, an absence that's been filled, still leave a mark? How can it reduce me to this? And yet, somehow, it does. It's just like when I was twelve. A complicated longing. A feeling of guilt and shame. A bird beating its head against a windowpane. Heathcote has, so far, been a dizzying force in my life. The last two decades have been punctuated by his sudden disappearances, for which I've increasingly come to blame myself. I haven't been interesting enough, or clever enough, or perhaps I've been irrevocably tainted by having allowed myself to be adopted into a wealthy family. I am in some way bad, perhaps even evil. Deep down, what I really want is for him to disabuse me of these notions, to explain why it's all been his fault rather than mine. It's another fantasy of flight: flight from my own guilty conscience. I carry on driving down the blurry road. He can't see me like this.

I try again the next day. This time I keep it together as I pass the house. I park the car, step out, and walk slowly back down the street. I'm not the same person he last met, that bright and generally happy twelve-year-old who simply wanted to get to know the magical-sounding man who brought him to life. I'm a tall, skinny, somewhat confused, somewhat troubled, young adult. I still want to get to know Heathcote, I'm still charmed by him, but this time I'm looking for answers too.

Heathcote's house sits in a terraced row on a quiet street. Its small front yard is enclosed by a white picket fence, the paint only peeling away from the wood a little. White and purple hollyhocks have sprung up from between cracks in the concrete, swaying ponderously in the light summer breeze. The front door is white too and, I notice uneasily, slightly ajar. I knock and step in, completely unsure as to what I am going to discover on the other side. I emailed Heathcote to tell him I was in town, and asked if I could drop in, but I got no reply. I don't think the door is unlocked because I'm expected.

I find myself in a shadowy corridor with heavy oil paintings pressing in from the walls. In front of me is a darkened set of wooden stairs, each step holding piles of books and letters.

"Who's there?" a gruff voice calls down.

"It's Charlie," I shout back. "Your son."

"Oh right," the voice says. "Well . . . why don't you go through into the kitchen and I'll be down."

I follow the voice's instructions, passing through a book-lined living room into the kitchen, which is bright and full of flies. There is evidence of a cat. Its food seems to have been thrown into a pile on the floor rather than placed in a bowl. Out back, a long and wild-looking garden stretches out, anarchic bursts of green overtaking the path and making a mockery of order.

I'm just beginning to suspect that Heathcote has escaped out of a window when I finally hear him clomping down the stairs. He seems to have shrunk by two or three feet since I last saw him, a trick of perspective as I now tower over him. He's certainly grown fatter, however. His paunch bulges out from beneath a grubby black shirt, overhanging the leather belt that keeps up his brown corduroy trousers. He's grayer too, his shock of hair more ash than coal. The eyes are the same, though, shiny as jet and clever behind his rounded lenses.

From the pocket of his shirt he pulls a five-pound note and holds it out in front of him with both hands as he advances toward me, like an exorcist brandishing a Bible. He slowly and carefully tears the note. First in half, then quarters, then he places the fragments in the palm of my hand and closes my fingers over the top. When I open them, the torn fragments have resolved into a brand-new fifty-pound note.

"And that," Heathcote says, "is why I don't trust banks."

He looks at me a little nervously as I hold the note in my hand, clearly reading my mind as I wonder if this is perhaps supposed to be twenty late birthday and Christmas presents rolled into one.

"I, er, I need that back, actually," he says. "Quite skint."

Over tea and biscuits we chat—or rather, Heathcote does. Just like last time, he is brimming with magic and stories, which is charming for a while. But before long I start to feel like I'm being hoodwinked. I haven't come here to listen to a well-polished anecdote about the time he imprisoned one of Derek Jarman's assistant directors in a toilet cubicle for three days. These are, I feel, stories he could be telling anyone, stories I suspect he has told many times before. They have nothing at all to do with the current situation. As with his magic tricks, he's running on a well-rehearsed script, simultaneously showing off and hiding, throwing sand in my eyes once again.

An enormous bluebottle buzzes through the air between us. I clap my hands to squash it but it shoots away, returning to hover noisily around our ears. Heathcote, for the first time since I've arrived, demonstrates a display of concern.

"You can't kill it," he says, getting up to show me a humane fly catcher that he's built using two kitchen strainers and an extendable arm. He tracks the insect's flight path for a moment, then shoots out the arm and the strainers clamp together around the fly, enclosing it in a globe of metal mesh. He opens the back door, gently shakes the fly out into the garden, and we both watch as it immediately buzzes back into the house.

I sense an opportunity to take control of the conversation and decide to start at the very beginning. Why did Heathcote go from being an involved and loving father one day to a raving lunatic the next—what happened to him that night in that pig farmer's cottage in Cornwall?

"What do you mean what happened?" Heathcote says. "Nothing happened. It was your mother. I'd just had enough of her, so I left. She was young and pretty and very insistent and I was attracted to her, I suppose, but after a while, well . . ."

I try to take this in. No breakdown. Heathcote just horny old goat who got bored. My mother the mad one. Something doesn't quite add up.

"What about me?" I say.

"Well, you were an accident."

This isn't news to me, of course. But the way Heathcote delivers this information brings my line of questioning to a halt. Why, his logic seems to run, should he take any responsibility for an accident? This is a man who will accept no blame, offer no deeper explanations. Heathcote doesn't seem to have any desire to continue the conversation, either. His chatter falters and eventually he looks at me in silence, his eyes begging me to leave.

I step out into the street much more confused than when I arrived. I haven't been given the absolution I was hoping for. My mother has been lying to me all my life. No, that's not right. Heathcote is lying to me. Or else he faked his breakdown to escape the horror of family life. What was it about us that was so intolerable? *I did it. My fault.*

I can't explain exactly why, but this meeting throws me into a tailspin. My mum is fascinated to hear I've been to visit Heathcote and fishes for details, but again I find I don't have very much to say. I feel emptied out. I probe myself for feelings and discover that I have none at all.

What happens next is hard to understand. The rational part of my brain takes a very long time-out, although, sadly for me, the part of my brain responsible for memory does not. It's like watching a car crash in slow motion. A psychological self-immolation begins, one that seems to progress in very definite and increasingly destructive stages before total burnout occurs.

First comes the vacuum. Empty space. My feeling of hollowness metastasizes into a black hole, as if an entire world had been sucked out of me. Back at university after the summer, I find I can't interest myself in anything. I stop going to lectures entirely. In mandatory tutorials, when I manage to turn up, I struggle to string sentences together. I'm aware that something has gone wrong, but I don't seem to be able to do anything about it. All I can do, in fact, is make things worse. I try to fill the hole, try to create feeling, but all I succeed in doing is passing through the black hole and entering stranger space.

The next stage: mania. This is a place I cannot revisit without paying a heavy price. I begin to lose control. My thoughts and actions jog out of kilter with reality. My behavior becomes random and erratic. I'm still trying to make things better, but each time I try I succeed only in making things worse. I know that all this has something to do with Heathcote. That if I could make him come to me, somehow, then normality would reign once again. I become obsessed with the idea that he should attend my twenty-first birthday party. I email him about it repeatedly—if he comes, I write, it will make up for everything. Heathcote does not seem to think he has anything to make up for.

On the day of my birthday, I've already been awake for two days, and I turn up hours late to the restaurant. My mum is shocked to see the state I'm in. I haven't been home much since summer and the change is stark. My relationship with drugs—already intimate—has become deeply committed: something close to self-harm. Self-abuse. My skin has turned a sickly shade of yellow. There are enormous bags under my eyes. I've lost weight. The words coming out of my mouth make very little sense. I spend much of the dinner hiding underneath the table. It's bad, but it's only a dress rehearsal for what's to come.

As my behavior grows wilder, so do my thoughts. It's obvious I'm cracking up, but that's not how I feel. I feel enormously powerful.

Supernaturally powerful. And maybe I am. Maybe I really do have the power to cause accidents with my mind; maybe I really am king of an invisible empire. Or maybe these are the telltale signs of a burgeoning drug psychosis that I am entirely unable to see.

That fall, there's a wave of student protest against the government. My university and dozens of others go into occupation; students take control of faculty buildings and squat in them for weeks in protest at the government's plan to raise tuition fees. Rule books are tossed from the windows and I am drawn to the chaos like a kitten to a ball of yarn. It hardly needs to be said that I am far from a blessing to the student movement. I turn up to meetings drunk or high, eat all the communal food, needlessly provoke the police, and make unhelpful suggestions: Let's nail all the doors in the university shut; let's set fire to the Senate House, an eighteenth-century ceremonial hall constructed mostly from incombustible stone. The sober, sane students around me prepare for the important demonstration that's coming up in London by stitching banners and painting signs. I shave off the hair around my temples to let space particles supercharge my brain. I am, I've decided, the movement's secret weapon.

By the time of the protest, a few weeks before Christmas, I'm truly deranged. I've never looked worse, or been more unwell in my life but, perversely, I've never felt better. I feel fantastically alive. Zingy and immortal. Possessed of maniacal energy and messianic purpose. I believe I have the power to bring down the government, perhaps even to raze and rebuild the entire British state. I can upturn rules with a thought and have flashes of inspiration that cannot be disobeyed. So far this morning, in the service of this chaotic mission, I've let myself into the back of an ambulance in search of morphine; tried to kidnap a rat-faced male academic with a fruit knife; and woken up a friend of a friend with a broken chain saw demanding a full English breakfast. Nothing unusual, all par for the course. Now on the tube to Westminster I waggle the sharp prongs of a pair of stolen surgical pliers under the noses of the other passengers, loudly and excitedly explaining that I'm going to Parliament to extract Nick Clegg's teeth. Things really go downhill from there.

In my pocket I have a packet of prescription tranquilizers, strong blue ones, which I keep swallowing with swigs of cooking brandy. On some level I must be aware that I need to stop myself, but the pills don't seem to be calming me down—quite the opposite, in fact. Despite the lack of sleep, the lack of food, the alcohol, and all the drugs, I emerge from the station at a sprint. I charge into a branch of Pizza Express, seize a yellow carnation from somebody's table, and throw it to the floor. The revolution, I inform the diners and staff, has begun.

I don't stop to watch the effect my words have on the people. As they undoubtedly toss their aprons and napkins in the air and pile out into the street, I race ahead of them toward Parliament Square. I haven't forgotten about my dental appointment with the leader of the Liberal Democrats. To my eyes, Parliament glows like a great beacon on a sea of emeralds, like a flame on a hill. Because of drugs? Sleep deprivation? The warped refraction of the world through a splintered mind? Impossible to say. I charge toward it, shouting and raving, and the crowd miraculously parts before me as if I am Moses. The double-reinforced lines of riot police do not, however. I bounce off their shields and truncheons and fall back into the crowd. I sprint everywhere. This energy will not leave me. I attempt a one-man raid on Westminster Abbey. I try to set fire to the Supreme Court. I arrive on Whitehall and there I see it, the key I didn't even know I was looking for, a great stone button rising from the middle of the road with levers and flags fixed to its sides. This object, I know, is one of great power, and I can harness that power to make Parliament disappear. The fact that it's the Cenotaph, the most somber memorial to Britain's war dead, doesn't even enter my consciousness. All I can think about is my own urgent mission. I run toward it at full speed, leap up the side, and grab hold of the thick Union Flag hanging down. I push off like a rappeller and swing wildly back and forth, springing and shouting, totally certain that what I'm doing is good. Unobserved by me, a press photographer snaps away.

That is just the beginning. As the day darkens, so does the protest. Masked groups go around smashing in the windows of businesses belonging to tax dodgers. Riot police smash skulls. A mounted policeman drags a friend along by her hair and throws her onto a curb. Prince Charles attempts to drive his Rolls-Royce through town to get to the opera and finds himself surrounded. I wave at him through the window and I swear to God he waves back. I jump onto the hood of one of his security cars and give the mob the royal wave. I *am* the King.

With the miniature Cenotaph in my hand, I feel a residual flare of that world-straddling feeling; a burst of flame across the cortex. It was like flying, like living a flying dream, no barrier between thought and action. Something tore on that day, and the tear still hasn't fully healed. I set the object down on the table. A somewhat unpleasant wedding gift. But perhaps Heathcote just thinks I'm irresistibly drawn to war memorials. That would certainly make more sense than the truth, which even I still struggle to make sense of. How do you rationalize the irrational? How do you reconcile a loss of control as extreme as that with the idea of yourself as a reasonable human being? To think that I did all those things is frightening. What's even more frightening is the fact that the part of me that did them is still in here, somewhere, resting.

The day after the protest, having somehow managed to get home, I tried to explain myself to my dad. I tried to be honest. I had power, but that power had somehow misfired. Drugs were the problem, I told him—they'd interfered with my power. He just looked sad. Small and sad and a little bit scared. Splashed across the front pages of that morning's newspapers was a picture of me hanging off the side of the Cenotaph—anonymous, but not for long. People were outraged. They didn't see things the way I had. All they saw was a long-haired student protestor pointlessly attacking a war memorial. Before the morning was out, someone had identified that student as me. Then the floodgates opened. "People want you dead," my mum said, looking blankly at her computer screen. "And . . . they want *me* dead too." Letters and packages with alarming contents began to arrive at any address linked to my name: my old school, my university, my family home. A black spot. A gift-wrapped dog turd. White powder. Death threats. Curses. Wishes for my entire family to die from cancer. I should be hoisted up a flagpole in Afghanistan and my mum should have her womb cut out to stop her producing any more bastard spawn. I'd placed a target on all of our heads. Then the police came knocking.

I look at the inscription on the front of the model Cenotaph and wonder, not for the first time, if I simply misread it. It wasn't the Glorious Dead I wanted to attack back then, but the Glorious Dad—perhaps. If it was all some sort of twisted bid for Heathcote's attention, a last desperate attempt to impress him, then it failed. He steered well clear of the disaster zone. David was the one who picked me up again, who stood by my side during the trial, and who came with my mum to visit me in prison. Who's your daddy? After all that, I finally knew.

The other object to emerge from this Pandora's box of wedding gifts is rather beautiful. It's a plate made by Heathcote's sister—a member of my family who, up until now, I barely even knew existed. At the center of the glazed terra-cotta is a hand-painted design: a man taking a sledgehammer to the hood of a family car. Heathcote's hatred of cars is well documented. He wrote an entire book about it and people I meet who knew him back when he lived in London often seem to have stories about him stealing, wrecking, or vandalizing cars. If the miniature Cenotaph is somehow meant to represent some aspect of me, then this is undeniably a representation of Heathcote's wilder nature. That the Heathcote on the plate is attacking a family station wagon, complete with roof rack and jump seats for the extra children, seems significant.

Both gifts are clearly imbued with personal meaning, though what the overall message is I'm struggling to see. Perhaps Heathcote is trying to point out the similarities between us. Perhaps it's a warning. I shudder at the thought.

After the episode with the Cenotaph, I realized I had to purge myself. Putting things into my body—drugs mostly—hadn't helped, but perhaps taking something out would. I clearly had something evil inside me that I needed to get rid of. I fantasized about going to the Somme and opening a wrist to make a blood sacrifice to the war dead, or about being flagellated in front of the Cenotaph by a pair of paratroopers—after what I'd done, I knew volunteers wouldn't be hard to find. Part of me craved punishment but, aside from a few inconsequential acts of self-harm, these impulses remained in the world of fantasy. I had to find another way to purge. In the end, I just stuck a needle in a vein and filled a syringe with blood. Before it congealed, I used some of it to write a very short letter, which I mailed to Heathcote along with the almost full syringe. The red letters smeared across the page spelled out a simple message: "Have your blood back."

That was my version of a cure. Not a wholly effective one, I have to admit, but it was the best I could come up with at the time. Send the problem back to the source. It was also the note on which my last attempt at making Heathcote part of my life ended. If his presents really are a warning, then maybe I should heed them. There's unsteady ground where the two of us meet. Cracks open up, for me and perhaps for him, too. I wonder for the first time if I am to Heathcote what this doll's house Cenotaph is to me: a reminder of a shameful, and frightening, loss of control. And an implied threat: Things can fall apart again. I decide to shut Heathcote out once more—no blood this time, I'm just going to put him back in his box.

In any case, a much more pressing conundrum is dancing around on the coffee table in front of me, picking and poking at the doll's house Cenotaph with an ebony beak. Benzene has come back with us. This, I hope, is tangible evidence that Heathcote and I have different destinies. His little crow flew away—possibly to its death. Mine, on the other hand, refuses to leave.

Chapter 20

Beak marks in the butter. A feather in the sink. Meat and money tucked between the pages of a novel. The magpie is making himself at home, again—this time, perhaps, for good. Our attempts to free the bird proved as futile an endeavor as trying to free a kite. We'll keep on trying, although I'm now less than certain it's the right thing to do. It could be that he's bound to us for life.

With this thought in mind, I hit the books. Can humans and corvids ever live together in harmony? It's a question that has taken on vital importance. How do stories like this go?

There are plenty of famous and unexpected examples of men and crows cohabiting—but contentedly? I'm not so sure. It turns out that Heathcote isn't the only writer to have lived with a carrion bird. The poet Lord Byron was accompanied by many animals on his travels, including a tame crow. The poor bird limps from one misfortune to the next across the pages of the poet's surviving diaries. First it goes lame after someone apparently treads on its toe—mirroring its owner's clubfoot but inspiring little sympathy as Byron later gives the bird a beating "for stealing the falcon's victuals." To misquote Lady Caroline Lamb, he was mad, bad, and dangerous to crows. Charles Dickens shared his London home with a talking raven, whom he adored, but his bird came to a sticky end after eating most of a staircase and a pot of lead paint. And Truman Capote was driven out of Sicily as a witch because of his pet raven, Lola, who later threw herself off his balcony in Rome, landed on the back of a truck, and vanished, leaving Capote eating dust and choking back tears.

As Benzene makes himself more and more at home in ours, I cast around for happier endings, although with little success. European folk wisdom warns against allowing corvids even in the vicinity of one's home. A magpie at the window is death; a jackdaw on the roof or down the chimney is death; a crow just about anywhere near a human habitation is death. And often misfortune does seem to follow in their flight path. Delving further back into history, I come across a woman by the name of Molly Leigh who kept company with a jackdaw in eighteenth-century England. Accusations of witchcraft followed and when she died, a stake was driven through her heart and her jackdaw was sealed alive inside her coffin. Marie Antoinette was said to have kept company with a tame crow; she let it eat cake from the palm of her hand and look what happened to her. "Raise a crow," one proverb warns, "and it'll peck out your eyes."

I drop the dead poets and the mythology books and start looking for answers in the material world. The truth of the matter is that we are all already living with corvids whether we like it or not. With their quick wits and adventurous eating habits, corvids—crows, magpies, and jackdaws especially—have been able to thrive in the urban environment. The booming human population has its avian shadow. According to some estimates, there are more crows on Earth now than at any time in its history. In some cities, there is estimated to be one breeding pair of crows for every two households or, to put it another way, one crow for every five humans. And that number is growing. Urban crows are more successful than their bumpkin counterparts: More of their eggs make it to adulthood. Corvids love cities so much they are even willing to commute. Studies conducted in America have shown that rural crows will travel as far as twenty miles a day from home to work, and in Greenland ravens think little of their ninety-mile commute from one garbage dump to the next. Cities, ironically, have become a haven for nature, or at least for species capable of spinning sustenance from human waste, which the crow family certainly is. This superabundance of food alongside the strict anti-hunting regulations in most of our cities has created a corvid exponential.

The magpie that fell out of its nest and into my hands isn't such a freak after all. Sick and injured corvids are falling into the paths of humans all the time, and sometimes the humans pick them up. It's probably yet another advantage of city living—access to free health care.

On the Internet, I've begun to infiltrate the fringes of a corvine community made up of people who have scooped these birds off the ground and then discovered, for one reason or another, that it's very hard to put them back down again. I've found a shy-seeming geek in the Midlands who divides his time between restoring retro video game consoles and caring for his disabled rook, crow, and magpie; an eccentric animal handler in High Wycombe who feeds his talking crow, Yum Yum, mealworms and toenail clippings from his own mouth at the dinner table; a wheelchair user in Israel who has trained her hooded crow to act as a helper animal, flying to grab things from high shelves; a young heavy-metal fan in Russia whose magpie fetches him coins on command; and a lady in Staffordshire who roasts a turkey every Christmas for her flock of crows—and has done so every year since her husband left. There's even a digital space where many of these bird-heads seem to hang out—the Crow Forum. Here I find much more useful advice than anything Byron, Dickens, or Heathcote have to offer. There seem to be all sorts of ways of living with members of the crow family. There are crows who have free run of the house, crows who live in aviaries, crows who are taken to fly free in wide-open fields on the weekends, and crows who visit the pub and go on camping trips dressed in odd little harnesses. Benzene's story doesn't have to have a sticky ending.

Having said that, life with corvids does seem to be universally noisy and messy. Debates on the forum center on things like which brands of dog food are best for attracting flocks of carrion crows to your back garden, or whether they in fact prefer bowls of fresh chicken liver; how jackdaws like their eggs (scrambled, no salt or pepper, with the shells crushed and mixed in, apparently); and what sorts of toys are appropriate for ravens (puzzles for preschoolers seem to be about their speed).

Benzene took little interest in my research when I was nose-deep in books. But now that pictures and videos of birds are flashing on my computer screen, he dances across my keyboard. I play him a video of another magpie—George, a particularly articulate bird who resides in a zoo in Alaska—babbling away to one of his keepers, and he presses his head close to the screen, looking and listening with rapt attention before deciding to launch a vicious attack, landing one peck after another on the image of poor George. A crow leaping onto the rim of a shallow bathtub and dive-bombing in with an almighty splash inspires more respect—reverence, even, for a master of the art.

On the Crow Forum I meet a kind woman who shares her home with seven magpies.

"How do you manage it?" I ask.

"We can't have anything nice," she types back on her droppings-splodged keyboard. "Everything gets hidden, or destroyed, or messed on."

I show Yana our exchange, but she doesn't find it especially funny. Yana likes having nice things and doesn't like my suggestion that we should just buy a few dozen glass bell jars of various sizes to protect the houseplants and trinkets from the magpie's inquiring beak. Ever since we came back from the farm, Benzene has been fixated on her precious orchids. Nothing seems to give the bird more pleasure than to soar into our room at dawn, tear an orchid up by the roots, and then scatter the wood chippings and soil in Yana's underwear drawer. And my jokes about how we don't need a baby because we have a magpie don't seem to be sweetening the air.

How to live with wildness like this? The magpie's energy is relentless; his appetite for destruction seemingly bottomless. In desperation I turn to another member of the corvine community for advice.

"Why don't you buy him an iPad?" she suggests.

The day I find Yana in the living room, hot tears of frustration running down her cheeks, cursing the magpie as he completes a victory lap with a prize bloom in his beak, is the day we agree the bird should start spending more time outdoors. The collective wisdom of the Crow Forum confirms my instinct that letting a tame magpie fly totally free in London is a recipe for disaster. So then why not build an aviary? A safely enclosed outdoor space for him to spend time in, where it doesn't matter what sort of mess he makes. And then on weekends we'll take him back to the farm to fly free, hoping he leaves, hoping he comes back.

So it is that a sort of corvid arcade emerges from the side of the house. I am all for enclosing the entire back garden but Yana, quite reasonably, disagrees. The magpie, she says, can have the side return, a strip of ground between the kitchen and the neighbor's garden fence that should be adequate to his needs. It only takes an afternoon to complete. My younger brother and I stretch galvanized wire mesh over wooden frames and pass them to Yana, who turns them into a slanted roof, then walls, then doors. It looks a bit like we've built a prison for our flower bed: ferns cower beneath the wire, and two waxy castor oil plants raise their hands in surrender. I count paces over the flagstones. It's longer and wider than any human prison cell, certainly, and relative to the size of the bird it's enormous—more of a magpie mansion than anything carceral. But considering the extent to which I have psychologically identified with this bird, it would be a little odd if I didn't feel at all uncomfortable about putting him in something that resembles a cage.

The magpie watches with some concern as I carry down the furniture from "his" room and pass it to Yana through the kitchen window. Out go his feeding table, his perches, his toys, the little plastic Buddha whose arms he has torn off, and the baking tray he uses as a bath. At the bottom of a wicker basket, buried carefully beneath a grubby dish towel, I discover one of Benzene's treasure troves. I pause for a moment. I feel weirdly guilty, as if my fingers are hovering over a friend's private diary. Curiosity inevitably gets the better of me. I close the door so the bird doesn't catch me in the act and upend the basket.

Pebbles. Lighters. Coins. Brass screws. Safety pins. He has the same aesthetic sensibility as an eight-year-old boy. String and sealing wax. I steal back a few of the things I want, and then take the basket out to the aviary too.

Benzene himself is harder to decant. He stands in front of the open window, swaying uncertainly like someone on the edge of a cold pool. I climb past him and lower myself slowly into the aviary.

"Look," I say. "Nothing to fear. Come on!"

I hold out my hand. The bird tenses. With his feathers pressed close to his body like this he looks reptilian: a lizard dipped in crude oil. He leaps, claws extended, and latches onto my index finger with a grip that is tight and warm. His head moves jerkily as he scrutinizes every aspect of this new environment. I walk him from one end of the enclosure to the other. He tips his head from side to side as he scans the floor and the sky for predators, like someone trying to shake water from their ears. After a while he decides it's safe and hops from my finger to explore. I leave the aviary and close the window behind me. Yana breathes a sigh of relief. Magpie out.

Chapter 21

Despite all our good intentions, we have failed, utterly, to evict the bird. All it takes is one piteous tap at the windowpane and one of us—usually me—will inevitably break and let him in. Even when he's apparently content out there, as he is right now, scrambling for spiders in the ferns and shouting at the neighbor over the garden fence, I often find myself beckoning him back inside. The sight of the bird behind wire makes my muscles tense up and sets my heart thudding uncomfortably in my chest. Even though it's what the experts on the forum have told us to do, I can't escape the feeling that something is deeply wrong. More than wrong: I feel trapped, hemmed in on all sides, and only partly on Benzene's behalf.

I turn my attention from the bird to Heathcote's wedding gift, the miniature Cenotaph, which now stands on top of a pile of papers on my desk. Wrongness emanates from this object too. As one of the only things I've ever received from Heathcote that isn't an autographed book of his poetry, it's precious in a way, but it doesn't exactly inspire cheerful thoughts. After the incident at the real Cenotaph, I found myself behind wire. Not in a psych ward, where I perhaps should have been, but in a high-security adult prison. Long before I even arrived, I'd worked myself up into a state of nervous agitation. A lot of the letters and messages I'd been getting from strangers in the eight months between my arrest and my trial focused in detail on what they hoped was going to happen to me in jail. "Your arse is going to look like the Japanese flag," one correspondent crowed. I was young for my age, and at twenty-one I'd be one of the youngest inmates in the prison. I told myself I'd make a weapon and use it if I had to, but I suspected I didn't have much of a chance. I had limited physical strength and somewhat feminine features—often mistaken for a girl, in fact. I comforted myself with the thought that suicide was an escape hatch that would always be within reach.

The judge found me guilty, obviously, and after he handed down my sentence of sixteen months, I was cuffed and led through a door that had opened up behind me to the dungeon beneath the court. The prison officers waiting below slow-clapped as I shambled down the stairs, skinny, pale, and terrified. They seemed grimly pleased to have me. The first memorable thing that happens after the prison van, after the enormous mouth of the prison swallows you up, is that you are forced to strip naked. Bend over. Pull back your foreskin. Lift up your penis. Show underneath your tongue. All armor stripped. Vulnerable as a snail without a shell. Prison clothes: thin gray tracksuit, no pockets. Then a quick medical evaluation. Suicidal? "Not yet."

The barrier between now and then is thin and permeable. The prison wing breathes into the present. The smell of cannabis smoke in the air, alarms, screams, the stamping of boots running up metal stairs. The wire netting spread between floors to catch the people who jump. A prison officer slaps a bald inmate across the head; another snoozes in a chair while on suicide watch; an inmate repeatedly slams his bare fists into a pay phone. A thought:

I'm dead. The only sharp object I have is a ballpoint pen. I keep it cupped in one of my hands, or tucked into my waistband, at all times, even at night. I don't know how much use a pen is. I'm not sure if I have it in me to stab someone's eye out with one but, even so, its presence is the only reassurance I have. The prison officers welcome me, in their own particular way. One stops me on my way to collect lunch. He wants me to know he has the power to perform a cavity search whenever the mood takes him. Later, another beckons. "Come with me," he says. "There's someone who wants to meet you." He locks me in a cell with a known killer. "He's asked me to break your neck," the killer says, smiling with his mouth but not his eyes. His eyes are cold and gray as lead. There is what feels like a very long, long silence. I measure the space between us, weigh my options. There are none. "And are you . . . are you going to do it?" I force myself to ask. He grins a little wider and claps me on the shoulder. "Course not," he says. "I hate that wanker."

One long month later, I get transferred to a lower-security prison where, I'm told, things will be easier. When I arrive, an inmate is screaming that he'll murder anyone put in a cell with him. A prison officer shoves me in and locks the door. My new cellmate glowers at me angrily, doesn't say a word until late that night when his voice growls from the darkness. "I'm gonna bite your fucking nose off, you cunt." I grope for my pen and sit bolt upright, as ready as I'll ever be. There's a pause, and then his voice sounds again: "Dada loves you," he says. "Dada misses you." He begins snoring. A sleep talker. No place and no moment is safe: Balanced on the toilet with my trousers around my ankles, someone rushes in wearing a balaclava and brandishing an enormous knife; sleeping on my cot, I wake to find a hulking great lifer, sixteen years into his sentence, towering over me and demanding a blow job.

It wasn't all bad, of course. There were drugs in prison, and I got a certification in art and design. A serial killer in the same class helped me mix the right red for the arterial spurts in an Otto Dix painting I was copying. It was possibly thanks to him that I passed, although whenever he picked up a craft knife or a pair of scissors he did make concentration a little difficult. According to a book about serial killers I found in the prison library he'd beheaded a priest with an ax and stabbed around a dozen more victims to death. There were moments of genuine goodness and beauty, too. Unexpected instances of kindness and tenderness that I clung to and tried my best to replicate. But the good is easy to forget; it's the other that keeps bleeding through.

The morning of my release came five days after my twenty-second birthday, on the same day as Heathcote's birthday, oddly, although that fact couldn't have been further from my mind. I didn't quite believe I was going to be let out. It'd only been four months. The rest I was due to serve at home, with an electronic tag around my ankle, and then I'd be on probation. Freedom by increments. Some of the prison officers hadn't seemed very keen on letting me go. In the days running up to my release, the frequency with which my cell was trashed by security officers performing surprise searches markedly increased. My cellmate, the sleep talker, who turned out to be a somewhat loquacious serial offender, warned of prison's strong gravity. "If you've been once," he said, "it's much easier to come back a second time. Prison pulls at you." There were, he continued, ways to deflect it. Superstitions to obey. Don't eat breakfast or you'll return for tea. And when you leave, whatever you do, don't look back—or you're guaranteed to come back. "And if you do come back," he said, "I promise I'll actually bite your fucking nose off." He presented me with a parting gift: a wooden lighter case he'd made from matchsticks, its handle embossed with a snake winding itself around the blade of a dagger. The symbol of healing, although not according to him. "Prison cuts deep and leaves venom in your heart." I thanked him, and left.

Out in the cold November sunlight, my parents were waiting in a car with blacked-out windows. They were overjoyed to have me back. In some ways, this whole thing had been harder for them than it had for me. There's no limit to the horrors the imagination can conjure up. And I'd been tight-lipped. In my calls and letters home I'd presented as rosy an image of prison as I could, partly in an effort to spare them, and partly because I'd decided never to admit that this place held any power over me. If I believed it, then it would become true. As the car pulled away from the prison, I turned around and looked back.

The bird lets out a rattling cry and I leap from my desk. Something's wrong. I hurry to the window. Benzene is flying through the air after a bumblebee that has foolishly buzzed into his domain. I watch as he snaps its life shut, stuffs its body into the crack between two paving slabs, and gently lays a leaf over the grave. Nothing is wrong. He's totally fine. And yet the sight of the bird behind that wire netting triggers a silent alarm inside my head. It doesn't take much.

I had no scars to show from prison—no visible ones, at least. The solidarity between inmates counts for more than the spite of the guards, and I was lucky that potential bullies never tried to call my bluff when I raised my hackles. The big mouth had spat me out unchewed. But not unchanged. On that drive home, we pulled over on a hill that looked out over the county. I stood in the wind and waited for a great rush of freedom and release to hit me. But nothing came. I felt as gray and empty as cigarette ash. No feelings, no release—perhaps because I hadn't really left. My mum noticed it first. The way my eyes darted around, never resting, always anticipating attack. I had a new outlook on life, one that involved constant, 360-degree vigilance, and a new motto: Paranoia keeps you alive. It was comical, really. I walked like a crab down stairs and escalators so I could see assailants approaching from either end; followed a zigzag pattern down the street, ducked behind lampposts, or else walked as close as I could to other people, to make it harder for someone to shoot me; scanned every single person walking toward me for signs that they might be a threat, and mentally prepared myself in case they were and I had to jam the pen still cupped in my right hand into their throat or eye socket. I felt like I was being watched all the time. "You're like a mad person," a friend observed sadly when he came to visit. "Stop asking why everybody is looking at you. That's why they're looking at you."

If part of my drug psychosis had involved a belief that I could harness the power of symbols, symbols now had an unfortunate power over me. The summer after my release, Britain hosted the Olympic Games and celebrated the Queen's Diamond Jubilee. The streets were full of happy people waving Union Flags and wearing Saint George's Cross. To my eyes, every single one of them was a potential killer. Anything to do with British nationalism, the Cenotaph, Remembrance Day, the armed forces, was a warning. Red for danger. All cars with remembrance poppies on their bumpers were going to try to run me over. All men in England hoodies were members of far-right organizations who were going to stab me in the kidneys. The revenge of the symbols. Some might say there's justice in that.

Operating on this level of tension, my fight-or-flight response went haywire. I alarmed friends and family by diving under the table in cafés or at restaurants or just running out the door and down the street, spooked by things they couldn't see, reacting to events that had happened months ago.

I should probably have sought help of some kind—for my sake and for the sake of those around me. Flight is a harmless enough response; fight less so. In the same way that the slightest thing could send me running off down the street, so my temper began to run away from me in a new and very unpleasant fashion. I didn't recognize the person screaming at the mildly obstructive ticket inspector that he was going to tear his fucking eyeballs out and use them as anal beads—but it was undeniably me. Me screaming like someone possessed, like someone who should be in a straitjacket, unable to stop. Me running as fast as my legs could carry me away from the British Transport Police. My former cellmate's prophecy nearly came true very quickly indeed—and it wasn't an isolated incident. I struggled to make sense of explosions like these. They didn't fit with the story I wanted to be true. So, I drew a circle around them and tried my best to pretend they hadn't happened. I should have talked to someone about it. But to do so would have required me to admit that something was wrong, and there was no chance of that. I was never going to show vulnerability or weakness again. I convinced myself—against all the evidence—that I was stronger than the state. *I stared into the abyss and the abyss blinked first.* Memories that didn't fit into this picture I simply rewrote. Thinking back, I convinced myself that I could almost taste the ecstatic rush of freedom and release I'd expected to feel when looking out from that hill on the way home from prison. But there was no feeling. Strong gravity held me down.

According to a well-meaning but unobservant friend, I'd undergone a classical katabasis: a mythical hero's journey to the underworld in which the hero defies death and returns with divine wisdom. I liked this analogy, but I must have lost my portion of divine wisdom somewhere along the way back. The truth was, all I'd brought up from the depths were paranoid delusions and an unpredictable temper.

These gifts from the underworld haven't left me in the years since. They've ossified into habits. It's only very recently that I've reluctantly begun to admit that something might not quite be right. That it isn't healthy or normal to keep a knife as long as my forearm on the bedside table, and another one by the front door, and the back door, and on my desk, and in the bathroom. That it isn't fair to the mailman to interrogate him through the letter box every time he calls. That the rumble of a van, or a knock at the door—or the sight of a bird behind wire—shouldn't precipitate a corporeal feeling of panic. Yana has been integral to this change. Her patience has kept us together. But it's the moments where she's lost patience that have helped me to begin seeing things the way they really are, when she's been appalled and embarrassed by something I've done, fight or flight.

Not that self-awareness is proving to be of very much use. I come away from the window, sit back down at my desk, and try to concentrate but it's no good. The silent alarm is blaring, and I don't have the key to shut it off. I catch sight of the miniature Cenotaph again and, cursing, sweep it into a drawer and out of sight. Outside, the bird clatters. I jump up from my desk, go downstairs, and clamber out of the kitchen window. The bird peers down at me from a branch above my head. I hold out my hand and he drops to it, a reassuring weight that fixes me in the present. The silent alarm goes dead.

Chapter 22

On the farm Benzene comes and goes. In the door, out the window, through the trees whose leaves are beginning to brown and curl as autumn sets in. The seasons change, but the bird remains. Like most of the family, his favorite place is the kitchen. That's where he finds my grandmother in her usual spot at the end of the table with a cold mug of gunpowder tea in her hand and the Saturday newspapers spread out in front of her. The carotene-tinged face of a billionaire reality-TV star, presidential hopeful Donald Trump, looks back at her from every single front page. He's said some new awful thing in his unlikely bid for the White House: Close the borders, screw the climate, shut Mexico behind a wall.

"Typical stupid ugly American," my grandmother mutters. She's never forgiven America for Korea, where she went during the war to work as a translator. She still remembers the smell of human flesh being burned by napalm—just like roast pork.

Without looking away from her paper, she slams her hand down on the table so hard all the crockery rattles.

"Got you, you little bugger," she says, flicking a dead fly onto the floor.

My grandmother is a champion fly killer. After Mao's very successful campaign against birds, China found itself with something of an insect problem. According to her, the campaign against flies sought to correct this. My grandmother was rather more enthusiastic about this campaign and surpassed her quota several times over, even winning a medal for her efforts. What the authorities didn't know was that she'd been breeding the flies herself from a rotting snake she kept under her bed. The snake was golden, and so were the flies that emerged from it, a fact that earned her extra praise. Benzene is immediately charmed. He too has passionate feelings about flies. He strides across the scarred wooden surface of the table and hops onto her forearm, bowing and clucking ingratiatingly. It's the smarmiest I've ever seen him. She beams at him—having long ago decided to make an exception to her lifelong hatred of magpies.

"What a clever little bird," she says. "Do you think he can talk?"

Magpies can talk. All corvids can, but Benzene has yet to say a word.

She thinks for a moment, then sees the newspapers in front of her.

"Fuck Trump!" she says. "Fuck! Trump!"

"Trump!" shouts the bird. "Trump! Trump! Trump!"

"Oh dear," my grandmother says. "Listen, Benzene. *Fuck* Trump! *Fuck* Trump! *Fuck, fuck, fuck* Trump!"

"Trump!" Benzene shouts, ecstatically pleased with his first human word. He struts around the table wagging his tail in the air and Trumping to me, to Yana, to the dog who whines and leaves the room, to my younger sister who cries out in horror.

After this, it's like a switch has been flipped. Back home, he spends hours standing on the faucet in front of the bathroom mirror conducting lengthy magpie monologues, helium-garbled versions of overheard conversations in which fragments of words are almost but not quite recognizable. Before long another crystal-clear phrase emerges from this alphabet soup. "Come on!" the bird says early one morning as I'm dishing out worms. "Come on! Come on! Come on!"

Trump is, of course, a word that everyone is pondering. The bird turns his name over and over in his beak, a weather vane for the world's anxieties as well as my own. Try as I might—and I do try, every morning and evening—I cannot persuade him to add the prefix of *fuck*.

It's the bird's other phrase that I find myself mulling over, however. *Come on* can communicate so many things: impatience, incredulity, exasperation, hostility even. The times I have said "come on" to the bird—while trying to get him out of the bedroom or despairing at finding yet another piece of meat hidden in my hair—might have been with any of those inflections. But the way he spits it back at me, with his high and bright intonation, lends the phrase a cheery quality. "Come on!" the bird says, dancing around on my desk. "Come on!" he says, calling to something inside me with an encouraging word.

BLOOD FEATHERS

Chapter 23

Winter has been a season of unexpected changes; changes that make me grateful for Benzene's ability to dispense encouraging words. Donald Trump has gone crashing disastrously into the White House and, a few notches down the disaster scale, the Trumping magpie has been banned from flight. He went missing on the farm over Christmas and I received a stern warning from the experts on the Crow Forum that he would perish in the wild. According to them, he is so tame, so humanized, that his survival, even somewhere as fruitful as the farm, would be unlikely. He must not fly outside again, for his own well-being. This news is troubling. We thought we were doing something good when we took the bird in. But maybe it's not so simple. If what they say is true, he might have to stay with us for life, whether he wants to or not. A magpie in captivity can live for over twenty years. Not what I thought I was going to be in for when Yana brought that cardboard box through the front door.

The most significant change of all, however—at least in the version of the universe that has me at its center—is that I have agreed with Yana to try for a baby. I know it makes sense, rationally. I want to have a child at some point, and Yana's argument that the longer we wait the more likely there are to be complications is a hard one to brush aside. Intellectually, I'm on board—emotionally, not so much. The truth is, I'm still allowing my internal compass to be guided by fear. Worst-case scenarios. Imagined catastrophes. The possibility that Yana might leave me if I say no—not that she's even so much as hinted at this—seems a much more immediate catastrophe than the distant and theoretical catastrophe that could be sown by a baby. Sensible thoughts about the actual reality of fatherhood elude me. That white-hot orb of terror is still exactly where I left it, blocking my path. So, I've given myself until July, around the time of Yana's birthday, to put all my hang-ups to rest. It's February now. So less than six months. Perhaps an optimistic target for a lifetime's worth of barely examined emotions, but there you go. Nothing like a deadline to put fire under your fingertips.

It's in this spirit that I'm off to see Heathcote this evening. He has been oddly solicitous since the wedding. The miniature Cenotaph was just the vanguard. Books (his, of course), invitations to his events, and kind notes about things I've written have all followed. In my anger, I've been dismissing them as self-serving attempts to assuage his guilty conscience—and perhaps in part they are, but he's clearly trying too, trying as best he can to patch things over.

His most recent invitation arrived with a copy of his new book, a collection of anti-American poems frighteningly illustrated with a picture of Donald Trump as an enormous pig. Before we leave, I open it at random and read a passage aloud to Yana.

The business of America is business
And its number one business is war.
Using Hollywood to peddle its values
It turns the world into its whore.

"Did he really need to abandon his family to concentrate on writing stuff like *that*?" Yana says, shaking her head.

The card he's written is sweet, though, and I feel a twinge of guilt for mocking him now, and for having ignored his previous overtures. He's no longer signing himself "Dad," I notice. Perhaps this time we'll finally be able to talk things over. Now more than ever, as I face the possibility of my own fatherhood, I feel like I need to know what happened. Why did he disappear? What made him run away? And there's the mystery of the jackdaw, too. How was he able to care for a bird, when he failed with a baby?

On the way to the launch, at a lesser-known members' club in Soho, my resolve starts to slip. I think about the popular definition of *insanity* as repeating the same action over and over again expecting a different result. In the past, trying to have a conversation with Heathcote has felt like talking to the magpie. It doesn't matter what you say, you just get the same well-practiced words trumpeted back at you. I feel like I know exactly how this evening is going to go. Heathcote will read a number of bad poems. Then we'll have a brief and awkward chat that will be constantly interrupted by his crusty fans. I'll suggest we go for a quiet drink or invite him to come visit next time he's in town or ask if I can visit him. He'll quickly make his excuses and leave. I suddenly get the urge to get off the train at the next station and head back home but Yana stops me.

"You've got to at least try," she says. "You'll feel worse if you don't."

We get off at Tottenham Court Road station. Outside it's foul in a way only London in late winter can be. Greasy drizzle, fog and fumes, soggy fragments of the *Evening Standard* sticking to the soles of people's shoes like toilet paper. We cut down a side street and walk over wet cobblestones to a cramped and muggy cocktail bar on the corner. As we step over the threshold, I brace myself for the inevitable. The familiar crowd materializes before me. Lame-duck poets sponging off their girlfriends and honking old men who act like they're important because they once stood next to Germaine Greer in 1968. Heathcote's usual flock. But Heathcote himself is absent.

"He's not coming," says one of his followers when I ask where he is. "That guy over there is doing the reading instead."

He nods in the direction of a middle-aged actor wearing a spotty cravat.

"Typical bloody Heathcote," I mutter. "Never there when you need him."

"Not really. He's dying. Didn't you know?"

I'm still standing at the bar blinking at this when a woman I've never met before approaches me. Early forties, thin, nervous, face a familiar heart shape with a pointy chin and prominent cheekbones. Clever eyes. A total stranger whom I somehow feel like I already know.

"Hello, Charlie," she says. "I'm China. Your sister."

The familiar details of her face suddenly make very obvious sense. I see that sharp nubbin of a chin, those cheekbones, that heart-shaped face in the mirror every single day. China. My oldest sister. As a child I used to mythologize her and my other half sister, Lily; telling friends about my two "long-lost" sisters, as if we'd been kept apart by some sort of romantic tragedy rather than by choice. Split up at the orphanage or lost at sea; anything other than the truth, which was that neither of them wanted—or felt able—to see me. I already had more older siblings than I could handle, but the thought that these secret ones might be a little bit more like me was seductive. I'd tried to contact China in the past. Not very doggedly, because Heathcote seemed like the first hurdle I needed to clear. But occasionally, when I met people who claimed to know her, I'd ask for an email address or phone number. "I'll have to check with China," they'd say—and that would be the last I'd hear of it.

We embrace awkwardly. She's thin, bird-boned, kin. I notice that her jacket is soaking wet and get the impression she has been waiting outside for some time in the hope that I might decide to leave. We look at each other in silence for a moment, both wondering what to do now.

"I've just got to go and say hello to someone else," China says. "Won't be a minute."

I watch in disbelief as she slips away through the crowd.

"Does she have some *other* long-lost brother she's got to go and say hello to?" I hiss to Yana.

"Oh shush," she says. "She's obviously nervous."

By the time my newest oldest sister returns, we only have a few minutes before showtime—a few minutes to catch up on twenty-eight years. It's a wide gap to bridge and only the most basic information makes it across. China. Lawyer. Three kids. West London. It's not an immediate connection. I'm feeling a little thrown: I came here to interrogate my father, and I've been presented with my sister instead. And oh, by the way, the father is dying.

"How's Heathcote?" I force myself to ask.

"Not very well," China says. "Not very well at all."

There's no time to ask more. The lights are being dimmed and the man in the spotty cravat is standing up and clearing his throat. We swap numbers and agree to meet again soon.

Chapter 24

I don't text China for two weeks. I'm half hoping she'll be the first to break the silence, and half afraid she won't reply if I do. I can't work out why it took her so many years to come say hello—or what can possibly have changed to make her want to see me now. At the back of my mind I hear the nasal voice of the man at Heathcote's reading: "He's dying. Didn't you know?"

Clearly something has given way because when I eventually work up the courage to send her a message, her reply is as friendly as can be. Soon I find myself invited over for dinner with her, her three children, and our sister, Lily.

As I walk down China's leafy West London street, I realize I've been within minutes of her home hundreds of times. A boxing club I used to train at three or four times a week is a short walk away. She might even have seen me jogging down the high street on Saturday mornings, heading up a herd of rowdy kids from the boxing club, whom I'd somehow been given responsibility for. One of my adoptive half sisters lives a few streets over, as do two close friends. It's like we've been living our lives in different dimensions—in invisible proximity.

Stepping over my sister's threshold for the first time is like entering a hall of mirrors. I pass through a corridor cluttered with bicycles and football boots and into the kitchen, where four heart-shaped, impish, elbow-chinned faces peer at me with expressions that range from childish innocence to adolescent indifference to a strange mixture of suspicion and sadness on China's part.

China's kitchen feels very familiar, too: wooden hutch overflowing with chipped mugs, battered cookie tins, and postcards; houseplants crawling along the far wall above a crippled settee; kids' drawings all over the walls—a sort of chaotic but homey bohemianism. An oil painting I recognize as one of Heathcote's is hanging over a finely grained wooden dining table. A field of remembrance poppies with crushed Coca-Cola cans for petals, a not entirely subtle point about disaster capitalism, I suppose. Underneath it, China's youngest child, a little boy with a mop of blond hair, is coloring in bottle caps with a golden pen.

"I'm making treasure for my treasure box," he says, holding up one of his golden coins. "Would you like to see?"

Lily arrives late and flustered with boyfriend in tow. She's come straight from visiting Heathcote in Oxford—or "Dad," as she and China call him. Like China when I first met her, she seems nervous and wary. Lily gives me the sort of hello one might reserve for a neighborhood kid who has come to ask for his ball back after having kicked it through the roof of your greenhouse. I cycle through my various crimes trying to locate exactly what I've done to upset her. Perhaps some of my ill-advised attempts at getting Heathcote's attention caught hers instead. Or perhaps, I reflect, it's just the basic fact of my existence that's difficult for her. I am her father's faithlessness made flesh, after all.

Lily is the sister I'm almost entirely certain I've encountered before. If I'm not mistaken, we've crossed paths secretly and anonymously online. It was a strange episode. I was seventeen and looking for traces of Heathcote on the Internet. One of the places I kept checking was Wikipedia. I watched Heathcote's entry grow from a few sentences—a stub—to a short biography as people anonymously added bits and pieces here and there, details I never knew about Heathcote's colorful life. At some point, a contributor added details about his family life and listed his children—including me. And then, not long afterward, someone went in and deleted me from his list of children. It didn't seem to matter how many times I logged in and reinstated myself, this same user kept going back and wiping me out of existence, symbolically erasing me from history. I assumed Heathcote must have been behind it, until I traced the user's IP address and discovered that whoever had spent so long trying to delete me from the family had done so from a computer in the office where Lily works.

Lily squirms miserably under the bright overhead lights as China presses a tumbler of white wine into her hand. I examine her closely, wondering if it really was her all those years ago, but now doesn't seem like the moment to go over old wounds—not when there's such a fresh one to deal with. Lily explains that Heathcote has been in the hospital for a week with low oxygen and bad circulation; complications related to his severely advanced emphysema. It's a confusing picture. It sounds to me like he's falling victim to the sort of random failings the very old suffer just before they die, the last stretch of the circular staircase down which everyone staggers with increasing infirmity toward death. But he's only seventy-five. I think of my dad, roughly the same age and strong as an ox. And my grandmother, well into her eighties and still able to snatch flies midflight between her fingers. Heathcote *can't* be dying.

"He's really seriously ill," Lily says, "but he won't do anything about it. He's in total denial. The doctor has been telling him for months that he needs to keep active, but he just sits in his room—and now this has happened." I can't work it out. He's either on his last legs, or it's something he's simply going to be able to walk off.

China serves a dinner of roast chicken and the two sisters gripe affectionately about Heathcote's hopeless attitude toward, well, everything it seems. Their mixture of love and despair is fascinating to me. Sitting right in front of me is the answer to the guilty little riddle I've secretly nurtured and mused over ever since I can remember. What would life have been like if Heathcote had stuck around to be my dad? I've often thought it really might have been a little like being brought up by Fagin from *Oliver Twist*. He'd have taught me to pick pockets with an endless stream of silk handkerchiefs and life would have been a merry crime spree. Or he'd have been like Merlin, revealing the mysteries of alchemy and flight. Or Sirius Black, the criminally insane wizard who escaped from a high-security prison to protect his orphaned godson. Part of me still holds on to this idea of a rascally old man blessed with supernatural charm and wisdom.

To my surprise, I discover that life as a child of Heathcote's wasn't all magic shows and mischief. Through China's and Lily's eyes I get glimpses of the reality of having such a mentally unstable man for a dad. Heathcote ramming a car drunkenly into the back of a fish van with one of his young daughters beside him, laughing hysterically as silvery mackerel flew from their boxes; being woken up on Christmas Eve by an earthquake and going downstairs to discover Heathcote in the basement taking a sledgehammer to a supporting wall, trying to gain entry to an imaginary room; the sense of relief when he was shut away in a distant mental hospital that could only be reached by bus once a week. Even the jackdaw seems to have had a sting in its tail.

"I hated that bloody bird," says Lily. "It used to attack me whenever I came to visit."

And that's as much as anyone seems to want to talk about Jack Daw. I think again about all the stories I've been told over the years about Heathcote the eccentric anarchist. These stories—about him drunkenly stealing cars from outside Notting Hill Gate police station, or setting himself on fire, or shoplifting Christmas from Harrods—always made him seem even more alluring to me. My imaginary father was unconstrained by the laws that govern mortal men. Until now I never stopped to think about how unsettling, how upsetting, it must have been to grow up under the rule of a man like that, at once so fragile and so destructive.

With this realization comes an unexpected flash of anger. Not toward Heathcote but toward my sisters. It would have been useful back when I was a confused teenager to have had someone to compare notes with, I think, gripping my own tumbler of wine. We could have worked together instead of against each other. It's irrational, and totally unfair. It wasn't their fault we didn't meet. Heathcote kept us well out of each other's orbits.

This meeting was never going to be easy. China's sweet children and her two cats ease some of the tension between us and I find my bitterness becomes more diluted with each gulp I take from my glass. My new sisters are guarded with their Heathcote horror stories—especially in front of the children—but they have both, I suspect, had a much tougher time of things than I did. I can't find it within myself to stay angry at them for long.

It would be an exaggeration to say that any of us feel at ease at any point in the evening. But by the end of the meal it's clear that something has begun to form among us. Not trust, or love, but a shared mission between China and Lily that I find myself being recruited into: help Heathcote. Just before I leave, China touches me on the elbow.

"You should go and see him if you can," she says. "Really you should."

On the top deck of the night bus home I sit thinking about China's exhortation as the city passes by in a miserable blur. All my anger toward Heathcote has gone down the hatch now that he's so dangerously unwell. I'd like to help him, if I can. But what can I possibly do? And what, a hurt little voice whispers, if he won't even see me?

The next morning I am woken by a familiar "Come on! Trump!"

I smile at this. I've been thinking all night about China's suggestion that I go and see Heathcote. It's been hard to imagine what I could possibly offer him, except guilt, but now I think I know.

After sticking the bird and his horrible breakfast out of the window, I sit down to write, telling Heathcote I've met my sisters at last and that they mentioned he's unwell.

"I could come and visit if you like?" I write. "Perhaps I could bring the magpie too, if that would cheer you up?"

I think about the magpie Trumping around his filthy kitchen, snapping flies out of the air, bringing a flash of color and life to the old man's dying world. We wouldn't need to talk about anything except birds if he didn't want to. All the pressure would be off.

Heathcote's reply comes by email a few days later.

". . . Thanks for the smashing card and for your concern. Yes, slight blip when I was reading an anti-Trump diatribe in a freezing-cold warehouse. The John Radcliffe [Hospital] topped me up and gave me a new certificate of roadworthiness. Back in harness. Sadly, there is an ugly feral cat here so birds are contraindicated. Come in the summer when it's not so damp and miserable, H x."

"A slight blip?" I mutter.

"Glad to hear you're a bit better," I reply. "I'd be happy to visit whenever. We could go for a slow ramble around Jericho sometime—or catch a cab to whichever spot you fancy—if that'd do you any good?"

Radio silence. I know I'm being tricked again. A week in the hospital isn't a blip and telling me to come in summer is simply a coward's way of telling me not to come at all. But I allow myself to be persuaded. It's a seductive story he's selling. He isn't dying, or even really ill. He's witty and alive as ever, just waiting for the sun to start shining so we can take tea in his garden and talk about birds.

Chapter 25

It begins with a hiss. For a second I think a cat's got in and is preparing to go to war. It's the same noise: a hackles up, fangs out, back-of-the-throat, boiling hiss. If it is a cat, it'll be out the window by the scruff of its neck. Just one bite is all it takes to finish off a bird: even if it escapes the cat's jaws, feline bacteria will finish the job. There are no cats on the farm this weekend, however. Fat Norman, my younger sister's corpulent blue cat, has been sent to stay with friends. The source of the catfight racket is in fact the bird—and it seems to be my dad who has inspired his ferocious song.

Benzene is on top of the fridge, somewhere he's been spending a lot of his time during this visit. It's the perfect snooping spot, his very own crow's nest from which to observe the comings and goings of the household. He's been rattling around up there among the bottles of vitamin pills for most of the morning, only occasionally swooping down to peck my mother's fingers as she tries to read the newspaper or snatch a piece of toast from somebody's breakfast plate; about as self-contained as he ever is.

But with my dad peering provocatively into the fridge, Benzene is transformed. He hisses like a goose and waggles his wingtips in an oddly alluring way. My dad looks perplexed.

"What does he want?" he asks.

Benzene runs tight circles of frustration, then scuttles to the back of the fridge to retrieve a precious piece of treasure, a shiny silver coil from inside a broken clock. He holds it above my dad's head and brandishes it as beguilingly as he can while shrieking, beckoning, and retreating backward into the dusty space above the fridge, clearly trying to lure him in.

"I think this means I've got some competition," says my mum.

Spring has well and truly sprung on the farm. Down in the woods, the first bluebells are sending exploratory shoots up through the writhing mulch. The crocuses have mushroomed miraculously from the soil and had their heads gnawed off by the squirrels. Pale blossom has fallen onto the brittle spikes of the blackthorn bushes like a dusting of ash on dark volcanic rock. And in the kitchen, an amorous magpie is desperately trying to seduce my seventy-year-old dad.

The hissing song starts up every time my dad walks past the fridge. It's unclear exactly what it is the bird wants from him and we all take turns trying to appease this demanding household god. A strip of beef; a mealworm; a dead fly; a radish: All are flung to the side. My mum, who for reasons best known to herself, has been trying to teach the magpie the secret of fire, even gets up to offer him a lit match. That too is tossed alarmingly behind the fridge. Yana is the one who eventually figures it out.

"I think he wants you to build a nest with him," she says. "Try giving him a stick."

In the wild, magpies tend to build their nests where branches meet at the very top of tall trees or, failing that, in the middle of hawthorn or holly bushes. In the urban environment, they will happily make use of man-made structures: nests have been observed on electricity pylons, telegraph poles, cranes, railway towers, and even inside factories. Magpies use humankind's fearsome reputation to their advantage: in rural areas they have been observed nesting closer to human habitations than chick-snatching crows are usually willing to venture. But a fridge-top nest has to be a first.

My dad—ever obliging—opens the window and snaps a dry old stem from the vines that cling to the exterior of the house. As he advances Benzene hisses, flutters, and finally lets forth a long, high-pitched squeal, beak open wide, thrilled that someone has understood at last. The bird snatches it and starts snowplowing around, clearing a space for his planned construction. Cobwebby old bottles of sunscreen and tubs of cod liver oil tumble to the floor as he lays his foundation—or should that be *her* foundation? Our assumption that Benzene is male now seems far less certain.

"I always thought he had feminine eyes," says my mum.

How does s/he know what to do? Other bird things, like flying and foraging, he had to be taught. This is pure instinct. He must have been born with the blueprint tucked away in some corner of that unknowable avian mind. Something in the air—spring or my dad's pheromones or both—has caused it to unfold.

Having previously had only a passing interest in sticks, mainly chopsticks whenever we try to eat Chinese, Benzene has suddenly developed a mania for them. He screams raspy instructions and we all go running for building materials, coming back with paper straws, kebab sticks, matchsticks, wooden spoons, and pick-up sticks. Only Yana thinks to go outside and gather some actual twigs.

Anything my dad offers is received with wide-beaked gratitude. When it comes to the rest of us, the bird is more discerning. Yana passes him a twiglet-sized offering that Benzene turns over in his beak, weighing it according to some inscrutable system of stick evaluation. Not good enough, he decides, and spits it over the side. My mum tries and is similarly rejected. "The bird's a starfucker," she complains. It becomes a competition. Who can pass the magpie test? He seems to like his sticks long and thin, although that's no guarantee of success. My younger sister receives only angry snaps in response to her efforts and storms up to her room in a huff. My mum fares little better. It soon becomes clear that the magpie prefers his nesting material to be handed to him by men, although how he is able to tell our gender when we have been so hopeless with his (or hers) is beyond my understanding. I sit back down and watch this strange communion between magpie and man as my dad quietly passes stick after stick to the bird.

The magpie is way ahead of me when it comes to the procreative instinct. I am still full of fears, both normal and pathological. But I'm slowly starting to become aware of something that was right in front of me all this time. I've been obsessed with this idea of bad blood; that I'm destined to follow in my biological father's footsteps; that I am essentially flawed, like the magpie of folklore born with a spot of the devil's blood under its tongue. What, though, if who you are raised by is more important than who you were created by? My dad passes another stick to the magpie. Always calm, always there, always ready to help. Not a perfect man or a perfect dad, but more than good enough. The bird certainly thinks so. He clucks and cheeps and thinks nothing of the strangeness of building his nest in a kitchen with a gray-haired human. If even a bird can adapt its nature—and adapt it so drastically—then why can't I?

For all that, it has to be said that fridges make very poor nesting sites indeed. They're far too smooth. And the magpie's methodology is hard to comprehend. He scatters at least as much as he gathers together, so frantic are his attempts to fold twigs into the fridge's unyielding surface. After some time, and much squealing, he manages to form a rough circle. And that's it. Construction work done for the day. He jumps down and gets on with his other business at double his usual speed, as if catching up for lost time. There is a pile of neatly ordered papers sitting on the table that he urgently has to inspect. A flower arrangement in desperate need of plucking. Nobody's pecked the dog's anus in a while. And what about all these flies?

It's always hard to wrench ourselves away from the farm. Now that the magpie has decided to nest there, especially so. But leaving a potentially territorial and aggressive creature on top of the fridge in the busiest room in the house by far wouldn't be kind to anyone. When it's time to leave, I catch him gently in my hands and Yana sweeps his skeletal nest into a sack. Nest failures are just part of life if you're a bird and I'm hoping he'll find it in himself to make another go of things in a new location, just like his wild counterparts would if their tree fell down or if they found themselves outmuscled by crows.

Back in town I waste a day in Yana's workshop building a wooden replica of my parents' fridge. For some reason I've got it in my head that the only place this particular magpie will nest is on top of a fridge. When I get home Yana is outside with the magpie. She stares at me through the window in blank incomprehension as I proudly gesture to the enormous and ugly wooden box I've lugged through the door. "Fridge!" I mouth excitedly. She rolls her eyes and points to a branch above her head where Benzene is nestled like a black pearl in a roughly woven bowl of twigs. *Of course birds prefer branches to fridges*, I think. *That makes much more sense.*

Yana reaches up and laces a long and supple stem into place while the bird squeals and makes forceful adjustments. This nest,

I realize, is not wholly of magpie design. Yana has been unable to stop herself from making little improvements here and there, adding plaits and knots no bird—not even one as clever as a corvid—could hope to replicate. I smile at this. I wouldn't dare tell a bird how to go about building its nest, but Yana has no such reservations. I dump my redundant box on the floor and climb out the window into the magpie's world.

"This means she's definitely a female," says Yana, as I pass the bird a stick. "In the wild all the males do is bring building materials. The females are the architects and designers."

I detect a note of pride in her voice. So far, I've been the only one projecting onto the bird, identifying with it to a degree that is quite possibly psychologically unhealthy: the bird as abandoned offspring, as an adoptee, a prisoner, a paranoid entity. Now that it's a maker and wannabe mother it's Yana's turn to see herself reflected in the bird's black eyes.

"It's sad to think she probably won't get the chance to have chicks," Yana says.

I mutter my assent. This is about the level at which our conversations about having children of our own tend to operate these days. Yana holds out a branch and I shrink away in silence. I suspect she thinks I've only agreed that we should start trying in summer so I don't have to talk or think about it anymore—and she'd be partly right to think so. But in my own quiet way I am working things through. The magpie's nest is an idea of family as faltering and clumsy as my own; an experimental thought delicately held together by thin shoots and bird spit.

Chapter 26

As April blossoms into May, the magpie nest outside our kitchen window grows dense and complex. Benzene takes what she can: Drinking straws, coffee stirrers, and chopsticks stick out at odd angles from her rough wicker ziggurat of twigs and moss. She has, as I feared, become violently territorial, and seems to believe that her personal domain encompasses not just her enclosure but our kitchen and living room too. Men are the only creatures guaranteed safe passage through the magpie's kingdom; many, in fact, are actively lured in. Benzene beckons to visiting male friends with wagging tail and fluttering wingtips, leading them all the way to her nest where she does her best to tempt them with a bit of human bait: an old train ticket, a stolen house key, or a scrap of tinfoil; objects that magpies apparently think we humans crave. Women are less favored. Benzene drives them from her airspace with a level of ferocity I didn't think possible from a creature that weighs less than a cricket ball. The last female friend who tried to step foot in our kitchen this spring, a somewhat sensitive moonfaced artist, left screaming with a murderous magpie hanging upside down from her fringe and trying to jackhammer its way past her fingers toward her soft brown eyes. The bird makes a few notable exceptions. Yana, her sisters, my mum, and my grandmother are luckily still thought of as family—but all other women, as far as the magpie is concerned, are banished.

Outside, the crows and magpies that frequent our street's back gardens are doing battle with equal fervor. The corvid-sized bird table I erected has become a fiercely contested zone, standing as it does on the cusp of two opposing territories. The pair of crows who have constructed their nest high up in a neighboring sycamore clearly consider it, and the scraps of meat, bread, and eggs that miraculously appear on it most mornings, to be their own private larder. The wild magpies, who nest somewhere out of sight a few gardens over, think the world is a common treasure house for all to enjoy. Whenever I put out food they shoot in like bank robbers on mopeds to appropriate as much loot as they can. They generally have five to ten seconds before the long claw of the law comes swooping vengefully down and the whole lot of them go tumbling through the elderflower bushes in the garden behind ours, the magpies' shimmering tails always just out of reach of the crows' snapping beaks.

This time last year, Benzene would have been an egg in the nest of a similarly lawless pair of birds; then a chick being fed stolen scraps; then for reasons unknown she was jettisoned over the side. Without Yana's sister having scooped her up, she wouldn't be alive. And without Yana having brought her home to me my life would feel very different indeed. Caring for this creature this past year has brought me out of myself, made me see it's not just catastrophe that lurks in the unknown; there's beauty to be found there too. These days when I leave the house I find that I'm looking over my shoulder less and up into the trees more. Of course, being tuned to magpie frequencies has its own stresses. Whenever I hear one of their rattling alarm calls it sets my heart racing. But at least I'm worrying about something that isn't me. All these things are causes, I decide, for some celebration.

Yana will have no part in organizing a birthday party for a bird. She is far too busy—and far too dignified—to engage in something so frivolous. As for me, work's hit a slow patch and I have very little dignity to preserve, so I set to it right away. Benzene isn't a difficult individual to please. Her medieval tastes are simple enough. She likes music, she likes men, and she likes to consume small animals while they're still alive. I arrange for a little of all of these, ordering in a box of her favorite wax worms and setting shiny bluebottles and glossy black beetles in clear gelatin to make a bird-friendly trifle that is at once strangely beautiful and stomach-churningly foul.

When the day comes around, the magpie vacates her nest and perches happily on the back of a chair, quacking along as we sing "Happy Birthday" to her. I blow out the candle for her and she plunges her beak horribly into the jelly, sending flies and flecks of gelatin all over the table. My dad strums her a song; my younger sister reads a poem; and a family friend, a venerable literary academic named John, unwillingly provides the sex appeal. This rather reserved man of letters is too polite to do anything but quote Shakespeare as Benzene places her birthday bluebottles and beetles lovingly up his sleeve and tugs the hem of his trousers insistently nestward.

For the non-entomophiles among us, my grandmother and I cook Chinese food, and during the meal she shows around a photo she's dug up of her with the sparrow she tried to save during the campaign against birds. I've always thought her rescue was successful, that the bird flew away—but no, it died, and even sixty years later my grandmother still seems upset. Perhaps because of this, Benzene favors her alone of all the women present, snuggling into the crook of her elbow and begging for flakes of pork from the end of her chopsticks. The only attention my mum receives from the bird is a vicious pinch and twist as punishment for refusing to hand over a cigarette. And when Sarah, John's wife, makes the mistake of lovingly touching her husband on the cheek, Benzene flies at her like a curse and whips the contact lenses from her eyes with surgical precision. An interspecies warning shot fired.

If you gloss over my mum, rubbing the back of her hand and glaring daggers at the magpie, and Sarah, crouching ashen-faced behind my grandmother in a pair of swimming goggles, and perhaps also John, quietly attempting to skim a horrible mash of jelly and insect fragments out of his cuffs with a teaspoon, this is a happy family scene. Afternoon sun streams in over the rooftops, the bird's tail a wand of emerald and gold weaving charms in the air. The color returns to Sarah's face and she even forgives the bird enough to snap a photograph of her shining scales. My mum grudgingly makes a present of her unlit cigarette.

A single magpie is supposed to spell misfortune, but the opposite has been true. This bird, with its relentlessly questing beak, has uncovered long-forgotten treasure. I keep thinking back to the last conversation I had with Yana about children. What about the noise, the mess, the expense, the inconvenience? She pointed at the magpie. When I thought of life with that noisy, messy creature, was the cost of worms the only thing that came to mind? I had to admit that it wasn't. With her, it's the good that sticks. The first time she spoke. The first time she jumped into my bath and splashed about on my chest. The time she secretly filled a Victoria sponge with crippled flies and watched as my younger sister ate it up. This moment we are living right now.

Chapter 27

Not long after Benzene's birthday, Yana's job takes her to New York for a month, leaving me and the bird alone. The beginning of Benzene's second year is mirroring her first. I throw open the kitchen window, expecting her to come tumbling gratefully in, but all she does is squeal orders for me to come out and feed her in the nest like a good partner should. She doesn't even want to come inside at night. She just squats out there in the darkness guarding what she's built.

When I post a photo of her construction on the Crow Forum the experts there congratulate us both. A nest is apparently a sign of a truly happy bird. She might even lay an egg, they tell me. She doesn't. She just carries on stacking sticks and trying to drag passing men up onto her branch.

We go on like this for some time. She trying to train me to fill the role of male magpie, me following her commands as far as my human form will allow. Each morning the sun rises through the newly reborn leaves of sycamore and elder. Its rays sneak like tendrils through gaps in the bird's nest, adding a verdant glow to her lustrous tail. I feed her worms and flakes of meat where she sits silently wishing for an egg. She preens and arranges her cushions of moss into ever more comfortable configurations.

And then one morning I notice that she's starting to destroy more than she creates. The same maniacal energy she applied to her construction work now goes into demolition. Each day brings a new act of vandalism. Tufts of moss are thrown to the ground. Broken weave hangs down like torn sinew. I try to stop her, or at least repair what she destroys, but as soon as I reinforce one wall she starts knocking down another. It's like trying to dam a stream with handfuls of sand.

One of my corvid correspondents reassures me that this is perfectly normal behavior. She's still young, he says. She'll get it right next year. But it's hard not to see it as a bad omen. Especially as some tragedy also seems to have afflicted the crows in the sycamore tree overhead. Their abandoned nest hangs down as ragged as the magpie's. It's tricky to explain to Yana over our patchy Skype connection quite why I find all this so unsettling, except that it seems connected to a wider worry that things are falling apart just out of my reach.

In the background, a human catastrophe has been brewing. In the time it's taken the bird to build and tear down her nest, Heathcote has quietly crumbled. He won't admit this to me, of course. His emails are as jolly and devoid of emotional information as ever. According to his version of reality, he's had to pop into the hospital a couple of times for a minor bit of patching up, but that's not important. The really big news is that a radical theater company is putting on a short play he's written about squatting, which he urges me to go see, and another play he's written about the power of song is being put on at the Brighton Dome. I should go see that too, he writes, pressing free tickets on me. The only time he confesses to feeling "a bit weak" is when I ask if I'm going to see him anytime soon. Despite his chirpy emails, I get the feeling that time is running out. He keeps putting me off. "Later rather than sooner would suit better," he writes. "When I'll have got my strength back."

My sisters, who have softened since that tense dinner back in late winter, keep up a parallel dialogue. In their world, Heathcote is clinging to life by his fingertips. He's been rushed to the hospital twice. Had a risky arterial bypass. There's a possibility he might need to have one or both of his legs amputated. His arterial bypass is leaking and he needs another risky operation. He is, China says, increasingly fragile. Toward the end of May she insists that I visit him—and sooner rather than later.

The magpie's nest is a tattered thing now: just a few broken sticks hanging down at sad angles. The bird seems to have forgotten about it entirely. She taps at the kitchen window asking to return to her regular orbit around my head. I let her in and together we hunt the flies she's been breeding in the living room. I don't know if her fly-breeding program is intentional or not, but the results of her hiding bits of meat around the house and leaving them to ripen are the same nonetheless. This sunny day on the edge of summer buzzes with heat and insect-wing beats as half a dozen recently hatched flies headbutt the windowpane. Seeing them, the bird shuffles eagerly toward the edge of my hand. She knows the drill. Like a game hunter riding out into the bush on the back of an elephant, she uses me as a sort of mobile killing platform, urging me to raise or lower my hand after the flies as they desperately attempt to melt through the glass. Their latticework wings stick cartoonishly from the side of her beak for an instant before she swallows them entirely.

Flies often make me think of that disastrous meeting with Heathcote when I turned up at his home looking for answers and left feeling as empty and worthless as his humane fly-catching machine. Our relationship has changed since then. We have one, at least, even if it's distant and slightly dishonest. I've changed since then too, although I'm not sure if Heathcote has. I'm fairly certain I know what will happen if I suggest to him that I come for a visit. So I decide not to even try. I'll just go. It might not be what he wants but perhaps, as his body unravels, it's what he needs. When China mentions that she's driving up to Oxford to see him, I ask to ride along. I don't know if it's more for his sake or my own, but I have to see him before he comes entirely undone.

Chapter 28

As the days get longer the magpie's discordant contribution to the dawn chorus comes earlier and earlier. She razzes me out of bed with her angry breakfast song at six in the morning, then five, and then my sleeping mind begins stitching the bird's cackles seamlessly into my dreams. As Benzene's cacophony bounces off the walls I press a pillow over my head and mumble something about catching crows in butterfly nets. This is my brain's way of pressing Snooze on the magpie alarm. She screams abuse through the door for a little while longer, then goes and busies herself about the house. Toothbrush down the toilet. Shit on the desk. Orchid into shreds. Beakful of bagel stabbed through the cellophane. I wake up late and gummy-eyed and follow her trail of destruction downstairs, where I find her ruminating quite peacefully on her branch outside the open kitchen window. I quickly scramble an egg, crushed shells and all, which I scrape into a bowl along with a drumstick and a handful of mealworms. No time for my own breakfast today. I give the magpie one last check to make sure she has everything she needs for the day then sprint out the door to the station.

It's barely nine o'clock but the temperature is already rising by the time I arrive outside Lily's apartment and my back is running with sweat. Both of my sisters are already there, waiting out in the street next to China's battered red minivan. I pant my apologies and then we're off. With the radio on, dried sandy mud in the footwell, dashboard ashtray jammed permanently open, and the tarmac in front of us wobbly with heat, I feel oddly like we're embarking on a family vacation. Cornwall or the South of France might be as likely a destination for us as a hospital in Oxford. Except that the family I'm with, these two sisters, are virtual strangers. The man we're going to see—our father—is probably at least as much of a stranger to me, too. As I watch the streets of West London slip by, I wonder who I know the least. Heathcote has lived and breathed in my head all my life, a sort of animated scarecrow constructed from secondhand stories and snatched encounters. China and Lily were only ever really names to me and, except for the little tales I made up for myself about them, they stepped into my life as total blanks—which perhaps frees me to get to know them as real people in a way I never have with Heathcote.

China noses her car onto the Westway, the clogged artery that spurts out of London toward Oxford. There are still so many questions I want to ask her and Lily—about their childhood, about how it was to have Heathcote as a dad, about our relationship now—but it still doesn't feel like the right moment. They fill the silence with that same mixture of tenderness and exasperation I noticed the first time I met them both. Heathcote won't listen to the doctor, won't learn from his mistakes, never bloody changes.

"Does he know all three of us are coming?" I suddenly think to ask.

"I told him we knew each other and were coming to see him," says Lily from the back. "He cried."

"Cried . . . in a good way?"

She collapses her face into a grimace.

Heathcote's ward is way up on the sixth floor of John Radcliffe Hospital. Out of the windows you can see the plains of Oxfordshire stretching out and melting into the horizon. The heat has turned up a notch—it's proving to be one of the hottest May days on record—and the landscape seems volatile because of it. In the fields huge agricultural machines beat the earth, rousing great clouds of dust. Red kites rise and fall on the rushing thermals, swooping into the hospital grounds to snatch sun-dazed pigeons as they drink from drainpipes.

Heathcote is propped upright in a wipe-clean blue chair by his bed near the nurses' station. He's wearing the same dark, sack-like shirt he always seems to wear. His shirt is dirt-encrusted and dusted with dandruff but, other than that, he doesn't look too bad for a dying man. His hair, even at seventy-five, is thatched thick on top of his head, an austere, steely gray rather than the long, dark, chaotic curls of his youth, the Heathcote of my imagination. Behind his reading glasses he has the eyes of one of those century-old Galapagos tortoises: ancient, wise, and smiling.

"Hello, Dad," China and Lily say.

"Hello, Heathcote," I say.

China and Lily each lean down to kiss him on the cheek. I follow their lead, brushing my lips against his papery skin. Heathcote seems pleasantly surprised. This, I realize, is a first. I don't know it now, but today is going to be a day of firsts.

If being confronted by the sight of all his children at once is comforting, or terrifying, or making him quail with guilt at what a hopeless father he's been, Heathcote doesn't show it. He doesn't even really acknowledge the situation. China and Lily gently steer the conversation, which takes much of the pressure off. With them here to moderate, things between the two of us feel easier than they ever have before.

Heathcote doesn't really want to talk about his health very much. Work seems to be all he's interested in. He's turned his hospital bed into a writer's desk on wheels. Every conceivable surface is covered with piles of newspapers, hardbacks, leather-bound notebooks, and poems annotated in that unmistakable calligraphic hand. He talks a little about his play at the Brighton Dome, telling me how it blends birdsong into the eternal hum of the universe. He asks China whether she can collect some of his research from home. He's writing a new epic poem—*The Red Dagger*—a grand celebratory history of rebellion from the Peasants' Revolt to modern times. At least, I think to myself, he's consistent: Birth or death, it doesn't matter, the work always comes first. It's his life; or his way of avoiding life.

Heathcote is, in every sense, still up to his old tricks. A small, well-worn navy-blue pouch sits on top of one of his book piles. As he and China chat away, I idly pick it up and pop the clasp: big, shiny magnetic coins slide out, one of Heathcote's many magic tricks. For some reason, my handling of these coins causes Heathcote immediate distress.

"Be careful with those," he snaps, a note of panic in his voice. "They're expensive."

I set them down carefully and Heathcote is immediately remorseful.

"I'm sorry," he mumbles. "I just had to save up my pocket money for quite a long time to buy those."

China and Lily both tut at him and roll their eyes at me. But from then on I notice that he has a charm or trick up his sleeve for everyone on the ward. He remembers the names of nurses and porters with a flourish, gabbles druidic mottoes in Welsh to the nurse from Cardiff, amuses the technician who comes to fix his respirator with a short discourse on the origins of oxygen. It all reminds me of the story he told me when I was twelve, about how he'd used his magic to charm a Turkish barber who he'd imagined was about to slit his throat. Now he really is performing for his life. No wonder he didn't like me meddling with his coins, protective talismans that they are.

Lunch arrives on a tray: sandwiches, soup, and semolina pudding. Heathcote suddenly needs to piss. He has a number of disposable cardboard chamber pots scattered about among his papers and reaches for one now without embarrassment. We all get up to give him some privacy. The doctor wants to talk to us in her office anyway. It's an open ward so I draw the blue plastic curtain around him as we leave, a small act that nearly kills him.

Behind the curtain he can't be seen. From his chair he can't reach the emergency alarm lying on his bed. With his weak lungs and dizzy head he can't shout for help. It's the patient in the bed opposite who spots the slick of blood—so dark it's almost brown—flowing out into the ward from beneath the drawn curtain.

We are ignorant of all of this as, in a quiet side room, the doctor explains the fix Heathcote is in. He desperately needs an operation to repair his arterial bypass, but she's not sure if the rest of his body is strong enough to survive an operation. A nurse knocks on the door and interrupts our chat.

"Excuse me, Doctor," she says, "a patient has become unwell." This strikes me as quite a funny thing to say because, well, duh. Then we hear "Urgent blood for Mr. Williams!" and rush out into the corridor.

The previously sleepy ward has exploded. So has Heathcote. He's gone off like a paint grenade. His shirt, his chair, the sheets of the bed he's now lying on are all soaked. A shallow lake of blood covers the floor. The medics rushing to and fro have left sticky red footprints and skid marks. Two nurses with thick forearms are struggling to contain whatever liquid is left inside him, pressing down hard on the blood vessels in his groin with slippery purple latex gloves. We are quickly ushered away.

It's hard to say how long we are kept out in orbit, the three of us revolving around his bed like moons. I have to go and cry several times. In an empty office, staring out of the oddly tinted windows at the depressing gray cladding on the side of the building; in the bathroom, hands gripping the sink; out in the corridor, with my back to my sisters, pretending to examine a poster about health and safety through streaming eyes. Tears always catch me by surprise. Especially now, when this man has done so little to earn them.

Heathcote isn't dead, not this time, although he looks frighteningly corpselike. His spindly arms, wasted legs, even his monstrously engorged feet are smeared with red. The floor is sticky underfoot as we approach the bed.

"I only wanted a piss," he jokes. "Not all this *gore*."

He keeps apologizing to the nurses for the mess he's made, thanks them for continuing to put pressure on his leaky blood vessels, but there's no charming his way out of this one. The specialist at the foot of his bed spells it out for us. If Heathcote doesn't have an immediate operation he will die; there's a significant risk that the operation itself will kill him; and even if the operation is a success, it will only be a temporary fix.

"I don't mean to scare you," the specialist says. "I'm just being honest. You'll probably have less than a year."

"Oh," says Heathcote.

As they're preparing to take him away, I realize with a jolt that this could be it. The last time I see him alive. If I want anything—

answers, closure, a stab at reconciliation—I'd better go for it now.

"Just in case anything happens," I tell him, "I want you to know that I love you."

I don't know if I even mean it. I just hope that it's a comforting thing for an old man with a guilty conscience to hear. He's loved; forgiven; I bear him no ill will.

He looks up at me in surprise, then smiles and winks.

"Yes," he says. "I . . . ummm you too."

I shake my head in disbelief. Typically hopeless. Still, he holds his hand out for mine as they wheel him away to the operating room and I take it. His nails are filthy, his knuckles are gnarled, but his skin is soft to the touch. It's a clever hand. Well used. Deft. This is another first, I realize, and perhaps a last, too.

Lily, China, and I step out onto the grounds and settle ourselves on a scrubby patch of grass in the shade of a sweet chestnut tree. China anxiously tears a sugared donut slice into shreds as we wait for the call. We don't talk all that much. I feel numb and removed. The call comes in sooner than expected, much sooner. Lily takes it. He's alive.

Chapter 29

Can birds read human emotions? I suspect they can. I cried for much of the journey back from the hospital: on the train and the tube, silently to myself. All that blood. His blood. My blood. Sticky underfoot. Heathcote powerless and vulnerable in a way I'd never seen him before, but still trying to cling to some vestige of power with his magic and his words. A dash of guilt behind the tears, too: Maybe we made him explode like that. Put him under pressure. I think about ladybugs and the foul-smelling yellow liquid they exude if you make them feel trapped. It's not their piss, it's their blood spurting out: reflex bleeding, the last defense.

Benzene is up and waiting for me when I get home. Poor thing. She hates being outside after dark. Rather than roosting on a branch like a normal bird, or sheltering inside the box I built for her, she's at the windowsill waiting to be let in. Normally she flaps indignantly to her perch without so much as a squawk hello if she's left out after hours. But tonight's different. She settles on my forearm and rests her head against my skin, cheeping softly. She even tolerates a few gentle strokes with the back of my finger against the fine black down on her chest.

Her eyes flash a pale purple-gray as she opens and shuts her nictitating membranes, a second set of semi-transparent eyelids. Their primary function is protection: a shield for the eyes that allows birds to hunt with their vision intact. But some animal behaviorists say they're used for displays of emotion too: A sort of magpie Morse code. She blinks long and slow.

In the morning, the bird's hideous squawking wakes me a little after dawn. Perhaps birds aren't so good at human emotions after all. I stumble out of my room to find a single black flight feather lying on the landing. There's another, a finely fronded semi-plume, halfway down the stairs. It's so light that its filaments seem to move in slow motion as I pick it up, like the branches of an undersea forest swaying in a gentle current. An object of delicate beauty.

Benzene has a jealous eye for beauty, too. She snaps the feather out of my hand and flies into her aviary, quacking happily as she lands on a branch and proceeds to pull the feather to bits with her beak. She pauses to scratch. Another drops from her body, falling as though through glycerine to the floor.

Her annual molt has begun. It doesn't happen all at once. She's a slow-burning phoenix. Over the next few months the old, worn-out feathers will come away in patches. Hard white pin feathers containing the new will force themselves out through her skin. Blood feathers, as they're also known. It's an uncomfortable process, perhaps even a painful one. She'll peck and scratch compulsively. But one oily-purple feather tip at a time, she'll be reborn.

Chapter 30

The day after Heathcote explodes, the same day the magpie's molt begins, I have to fly to Greece for my older adoptive half sister Sara's wedding, leaving Benzene in the care of one of Yana's sisters. It jars me to leap so suddenly from one family to the other, from one extreme family situation to another, and part of me gets left behind. The evening I arrive on the island there are sunset drinks on a terrace by a ruined amphitheater. The sweet musk of the village hangs in the air, the high smell of warm fig trees and piss-scented alleys combining with the heavy stink of donkey shit, moped engines, rosemary and thyme. In the amphitheater, goats ring their bells as they leap from step to step, stopping to nibble shoots that grow between the ancient slabs of stone. All of my siblings—the seven siblings I grew up with, I mean—are there. My brothers slurping beers in linen suits; my older sisters floating around in jellyfish-like gowns; Sara enjoying every moment. I feel like a ghost at the banquet; not truly present, a little grave.

At quiet moments during the weeklong wedding I keep finding myself back in the intensive care unit, a room as cool and still and blue as the bottom of the ocean, Heathcote's mouth grinning wide and toothless as a plankton feeder. Back in that moment, right after the operation, it's all I want to see. I'm trying my best to blinker myself to the human misery on the ward around us, but a father taking his newborn to see its comatose mother keeps breaking through my defenses. Feeling grim—but in a different way from China and Lily, I suspect. I barely know this man, a fact that carries its own weight as well as its own lightness; a guilty freedom from it all. Worrying that I'm just a tourist here, a backpacker who has stumbled across a family tragedy and decided to stop and gawk. I can't help but wonder if the sadness I feel is even personal, or if I'd feel this way after witnessing any old man leak a few pints of blood from somewhere between his legs. I half recognize this concern as being just another variation on a tired old question: Who is this man and what is he to me? What am I to him?

It soon becomes apparent that Heathcote is the only happy one. He is deliriously, narcotically, childishly gleeful. Without his dentures, his face has collapsed in on itself and in profile he resembles a wrinkled old cashew. He gabbles at us semi-coherently, then wheezes for breath and a nurse comes and fits the oxygen mask back over his mouth. The machines around him make reassuringly regular beeps and display softly undulating pulses. I have never seen anyone look so happy to be alive. The doctor's doomy pronouncement—a death sentence, really—has been forgotten for now. He beams at us wildly like a child who has leaped from a cardboard box, like someone who thinks he can cheat death forever. And perhaps he can.

Between fried fish and wedding vows I stay in contact with the other family. Lily seems to think he's getting better. He might even be able to go home soon, she writes. The sight of Heathcote so vulnerable, bloody and toothless as a baby bird, makes me want to do anything I can to help him. I offer to help find a caregiver or a live-in nurse so he can be safe and comfortable at home and ask if I can do any research to help him complete the epic poem he's been writing about rebellion. To my surprise Heathcote is not opposed to either of these propositions. Over the last week a quiet revolution seems to have taken place in our relationship. When I email him to tentatively suggest another visit on my return, his reply is swift and unprecedented: "Yes please!" he writes. "Looking forward to it."

Somehow, I too have forgotten about the doctor's death sentence. In Greece I come across a local legend about a sponge diver called Jonas who dove straight into the belly of a shark and lived to tell the tale. I relate the story to Heathcote in a postcard that I optimistically send to his home address. "Hopefully," I write, "by the time this arrives you too will be out of the belly of the beast."

Chapter 31

Back from Greece, I make my way to Oxford. On the drive there, red kites seem to mass above the car. I'm on my own this time so there's no one to stop me from craning my neck as I drive to catch a better view of them. They soar in groups, looming massively above the windshield like prehistoric creatures. In Shakespeare, red kites are birds of ill omen. They hover over the battlefield in *Julius Caesar* waiting to feast on the corpses of fallen men. Cassius describes them, along with their crow colleagues, as a "canopy most fatal." In my mind, though, they're a symbol of hope and renewal, of things coming back from the brink. After having been driven almost to extinction in the UK by the start of the twentieth century, they were reintroduced in the 1990s and now anyone who takes the M40 toward Oxford can enjoy the sight of these powerful birds of prey spiraling over the motorway. They are, I decide, a good omen.

While I'm pinning my hopes on the red kites, Heathcote seems to think that red grapes are his key to regeneration. Someone has told him that a certain chemical in the skin of red grapes can reverse his condition, so it's all he's asked me to bring. I don't believe this, but at the same time I badly want to believe it, so I've spent the morning sourcing not just red grapes but all other kinds of red fruits too. The passenger seat is bouncing with loose cherries, baskets of shining strawberries, and jiggling bunches of long purple grapes, delicate vessels for a dangerous weight of hope.

The sight that greets me back up on the sixth floor of John Radcliffe Hospital is crushing. Semi-reclining in a cot by the window, surrounded like last time by piles of books, papers, and mail, Heathcote looks out over a landscape made hazy by heat, as if the dull fields of Oxfordshire are gently simmering into the sky. He has aged dramatically in the last fortnight: his beard has grown out, wispy and gray, not quite covering his sunken cheeks; his lips have been thickly and carelessly smeared in Vaseline; and, I am horrified to see, bottles of Ensure line the windowsill. To me, Ensure, a thick nutritional milkshake, is as sure a sign of imminent death as the black spot. It makes me think of aged relatives dying slowly in the hospital—which is what, I forcefully remind myself, this old man is. Ensure is the food of the dead.

The old man hacks and coughs and then looks up at me with a grin.

"Sorry about last time," he says. "That was a bit of a bloodbath."

He seems genuinely pleased to see me, smilingly accepting the fruit I've brought him but not, I notice, making any immediate signs of wanting to eat any of it. With all the red fruit around him, Heathcote resembles a corpse at an altar, surrounded by offerings; a slightly simian ancient ancestor who comes to life when the light hits him in just the right way.

The ward, though it's full of sun, is a deathly place. There are only two other patients on it. One of them is fresh out of the operating room, having just had his leg cut off around the knee. As Heathcote and I chat, he writhes around in his pristine white bandages sobbing for his wife. He stops every nurse that passes and begs them to tell him where she is. The other patient, a stick-thin man with jaundiced folds of skin hanging off his face, stares straight ahead, silent and unmoving.

Heathcote doesn't seem to remember much about last time. He doesn't remember his wild ecstasy on waking up alive after the operation; nor does he seem to remember the doctor's cautionary words about how much more to expect from life. It was, he seems to have decided, a mere brush with death and with enough red grapes he can wash the stain away. He tells me a story I've heard a couple of times before, about how he's a member of something called the 120 Club—an organization of people who have decided to live until 120. "It's not a mandatory rule of the club, of course," he says. "Nobody will look down on you if you decide to peg out at one hundred." It's the same line he used in his last telling, although it carries a novel poignancy now.

I haven't spent much time thinking about what to say to Heathcote. I'd like to talk about the past, but I don't want to force him to go anywhere he doesn't want to, so I decide to let him lead the way. Even in this sorry state, Heathcote is an anecdote machine. Breathless, wheezing, coughing, talking at times like someone in a chokehold, he squeezes them out one after another. He talks about other near-death experiences, ones that have happened around him but not to him. He tells a long story about a fatal accident on a film set he was working on in South America, where a sixteen-year-old boy had his head crushed by a forklift truck. Heathcote claims he tried to give the boy mouth-to-mouth but found himself spitting out bloody fragments of teeth and bone. He tells me about how he organized a collection for the family and managed to persuade the director to dedicate the film to the boy. He gives me a sidelong look to see if I'm impressed.

Before I can ask Heathcote why, at this late stage, he's trying to convince me what a good person he is, he's on to the next story, this one about a past-life regression he experienced while being treated for alcoholism. A hypnotist put him in a trance, and he found himself in the Spanish Civil War having his tongue cut out as punishment for espionage. It was because of this past-life trauma, the therapist unhelpfully told him, that he turned to drink. Before I can unpack this, we've jumped through time again. Now we are in Edwardian England with his father training to fight in the First World War. A howitzer came loose from its chucks and crushed his father's legs, preventing him from being sent to the front.

"Without that," Heathcote says, "neither of us would probably be here."

Heathcote's father was, from the scraps I've picked up here and there, not a pleasant man. Heathcote Senior was an angry little Welsh judge who ruled his family like a tyrant. I don't know if he regularly beat Heathcote, but he definitely starved him emotionally, only rewarding him with attention if he was able to parrot Rudyard Kipling's "If." At a very young age he sent Heathcote away to boarding school where he certainly was beaten. When, later in life, Heathcote rebelled against his father's demands that he become a lawyer, they quarreled so violently that he had his first heart attack; the next one killed him. According to my mum, Heathcote always thought he was responsible for his father's death.

This is the first time Heathcote has ever spoken to me on the subject. Before he can leapfrog away onto something new, I grasp at the thread.

"Were you close to your father?" I ask.

"Not at all," he says. "He was one of twelve—can you imagine that, eleven brothers and sisters—and I think that made him rather competitive. They probably fought over how many peas they had on their plates. He certainly didn't like it when my mother treated me kindly. 'You spoil that boy,' he always used to say. He was an Edwardian, really. Victorian, almost. Very harsh."

The nurse comes in with a lunch tray: egg and coleslaw sandwiches, vegetable soup, and semolina pudding again. Heathcote thanks her, gives the sandwiches a prod, and then pushes the lot to one side.

"When I told him I wanted to be a writer, do you know what he said to me? 'How can you be a writer?' he said. 'You don't know anything.' From then on, whenever I came home he would just pour himself a glass of whiskey and turn his back on me."

Heathcote repeats the phrase, marveling over it: "How can you be a writer when you don't know anything?"

Heathcote's father died just before his first book, *The Speakers*, came out. Heathcote was twenty-two. He seems lost in fantasy now. He tells me about how, if his father had lived, their relationship would have been miraculously fixed by the publication of this book.

"If he'd read it," he says, "he would have been to all the bookshops demanding to know why they weren't displaying it in their windows. I know he would."

The nurse returns to collect the untouched meal and offers Heathcote a hot drink.

"Yes, please," he says. "And would you mind fetching a cup of tea for my ah . . . my friend here."

At the word *friend*, I suddenly find myself provoked. There's no legal document that can overwrite DNA. We're still of the same blood. I look at this man, this mess, still agonizing over his unresolved relationship with his father. A violent impulse snarls as the irony of him complaining to me about his father's absence hits. I want to shock him out of his fantasy world, to make him see the reality of his situation, how little time he has left. A dual desire moves me: a desire to punish and transform. Without quite realizing what I'm doing, I copy Heathcote. I start to tell him a story.

The story I tell him is about the process of human cremation. I've recently been researching it in great detail for a piece of writing I'm working on. I know it's a terrible thing to do but, once I've started, it takes on its own unstoppable momentum. I tell Heathcote about the 1400°F gas jets that blast into the torso of the deceased; about how the limbs start to flex as the muscles tighten and then all the flesh burns away; how the charred bones are scanned by a powerful electromagnet, which picks up fillings and hip replacements. The ward goes very quiet. The unmoving man with yellow skin rotates his head to stare at me in silent horror. The man with no leg has stopped asking for his wife. But I can't stop. If Heathcote is allowed to carry on pretending everything is fine, as he always does, then nothing will change. The past will just keep repeating over and over again.

"And then," I carry on, wishing the words back into my mouth, "they have to reach in with a special tool a bit like a garden rake and smash your skull into tiny fragments. Then they put you in a sort of industrial coffee grinder and whizz you up into a fine dust. Did you know you can choose how finely ground you'd like to be?"

"Oh," Heathcote says.

The nurse arrives with the tea and I quickly excuse myself to the bathroom. I splash water on my face and take a long look in the mirror. I haven't come here to torture a dying man. I'm supposed to be comforting him. Why does this always happen? Why can I never just say how I feel? I suppose if there's anyone who could understand this smoke-and-mirrors approach to human emotions, it'd be Heathcote.

"Sorry about that," I say when I return. "Would you like some cherries?"

"Oh, yum-yum," Heathcote says, taking one and hiding it up his sleeve just before it gets to his mouth. "Delicious. Thank you."

Chapter 32

As I walk out of the hospital's revolving doors and into the parking lot, I decide I won't be coming back here again. Watching this man trying to lie his way past death is too upsetting and frustrating. And I feel ashamed of having let anger get the better of me. I don't trust myself not to do so again. If, by some miracle, Heathcote survives, then perhaps we'll be able to rebuild our shaky relationship. But until then I don't think I have anything to offer him.

My sisters keep me up to date with his rises and falls. I try to get on with my life. Yana comes back from New York. Work starts to pick up apace. The magpie shrugs off her old feathers, getting balder and uglier as the days slip by. She's spending most of her nights indoors again, sleeping on a special plant pot perch Yana built and attached to the wall in the spare room. The idea was that her shit would fall into the pot and fertilize the devil's ivy growing there—which was a nice thought, except for the fact that magpie shit seems to be deadly poison to all houseplants. What started as a healthy vine is now a bundle of withered stems. She doesn't seem to have noticed that we haven't been flying on the farm for months. Despite having had ample opportunities to escape the house—thanks to my and Yana's forgetfulness with windows—she's only been out on the street once and, even then, she only did a few laps of the neighborhood before coming right back in through the front door. Her ideal habitat, I am beginning to realize, is simply with me.

Yana's birthday—the day we have agreed we'll start trying for a child—creeps closer but I'm still too entangled with the father dying in the hospital to think much about fatherhood myself.

On Father's Day morning, Lily calls to tell me Heathcote has taken a serious turn for the worse. His lungs are filling with fluid and he's been slipping in and out of consciousness. She and China are getting there as soon as they possibly can. I should do whatever I want, she says, no pressure; but the doctors are saying that anyone who wants to see him shouldn't leave it until tomorrow. I bite my lip. I had planned to drive to the farm and spend the day with my dad, but now I'm torn.

"Haven't you done enough?" Yana says. "It's not like he'd be rushing to your bedside if you were dying. If you'd had a relationship then it'd be different, but it's not like there are lots of happy memories you can comfort him with. Unless you feel like you really need to be there to watch his soul escaping his body?"

Yana's words are harsh. She can be unforgiving when it comes to fathers. But I have to admit that she's right. I can't see what I have to give.

On the farm, my parents are sitting out back in the shade of an old oak tree. My dad has a pair of binoculars pressed to his eyes and is watching a heron as it flies into a patch of wild bogland. The paddock in front of us is speckled with jackdaws and magpies. A buzzard circles silently above, waiting for food to run from the long grass.

Setting the binoculars down on the lawn, my dad opens the card I've brought him. "Number One Dad!" shouts its gold-embossed design. He snorts and raises an eyebrow. I still worry about him getting jealous of Number Two, especially on days like today when he is so very present. My mum, even after everything, starts worrying on Heathcote's behalf.

"Are they giving him antianxiety medication?" she asks. "He suffers from such severe anxiety. Tell them to give him some if they're not."

I check my phone compulsively throughout lunch, barely noticing the Sunday roast my dad puts in front of us. Lily had promised to call if anything happens, but my phone sits unmoving in my palm. I scroll through Instagram, blankly staring at pictures of other people's Father's Days while I wait for the news of Heathcote's death.

Eventually Yana takes the device out of my hand and leads me down to the river, where carp are sunbathing lazily by the water lilies. She strips and jumps in with a yelp as the cold hits her. The carp scatter. I follow slowly, lowering myself inch by inch into the golden-brown water until my eyes are just above the surface. I think only about what is right in front of me. A wasplike hoverfly sitting fat and lazy on a swaying reed. Azure damselflies falling like petals onto stems that protrude from the river, the tips of their wings dip-dyed with dark India ink. A dragonfly as menacing as a Chinook helicopter that beats its double wings as it hunts downstream. I ripple through the water, a living body unburdened by thought.

Heathcote doesn't die that day. He regains consciousness. He even starts working on his poems again. If he just manages to eat something and starts getting his strength back, he might be able to go home. The doctor's death sentence—a year to live—is starting to look like a goal to aim for.

The next weekend Lily calls again. The doctors are saying it's now or never. The finality of this breaks my resolve and, in the evening, with Yana beside me, I drive to the hospital in Oxford for the last time.

Heathcote is hooked up to a breathing machine as noisy as an extractor fan. It's forcing oxygen into his lungs; the air pressure keeps his collapsing bronchial tubes open. China and the kids are gathered on one side; Lily stands on the other.

"Sorry I missed Father's Day," I say to the old man in the bed. He cackles toothlessly through his transparent mask.

I sit down and give Heathcote's cold hand a squeeze. He looks up at me and squeezes my hand back. China tries to remind him of the happy times they've had together. She conjures up a memory of a magic show he put on for her eighth birthday. China's kids remember him transforming feathers and glue into fudge. Lily doesn't say much, and I, of course, have nothing to add. I get a sad feeling that the stock of happy memories is a bit of a shallow barrel.

Before long, China has to take the kids away to put them to bed, leaving just Lily, Yana, and me on the sleepy ward. Heathcote gestures for his mask to be removed.

"I . . . I . . . ," he says.

"What're you trying to say, Dad?" Lily asks. "Are you trying to say 'I love you'?"

Heathcote narrows his eyes. With all the force his collapsing lungs can muster he wills the words out of his mouth.

"I . . . I . . . Ice cream," he hisses.

Lily looks momentarily distraught, then her face hardens. It's all he cares about now, she tells me. Mango ice cream. She flags down a nurse who goes off to fetch him one from the staff fridge. The nurse returns with a melting Solero that she hands to Yana. Heathcote leers at her greedily and chomps his gums.

Yana looks a little uncomfortable. She and Heathcote have only met once before, very briefly. They're definitely not on hand-feeding terms. But Heathcote's wishes are clear. Yana holds the pop uncertainly to his toothless maw and he laps it up, slurping and sucking away without a hint of embarrassment. In fact, as he licks his way down to the wet wood of the stick, he looks up at Yana—to him, basically a beautiful stranger—with a degree of pleasure that is quite unseemly, a rather entitled baby bird, and more than a little seedy.

After this Heathcote is on a sugar high. He's a lot of fun in his own delirious way. He shouts instructions for the completion of a poem about the Cerne Abbas Giant's enormous erection; calls for more ice cream; for his tax returns; for someone to bring him a photograph of his father standing next to an ugly woman. Eventually an exasperated nurse tries to shush him; other patients are sleeping, she explains.

"They're not sleeping!" Heathcote shouts. "They're just pretending to be dead!"

With all the ice cream and excitement, it feels a bit like we're having a party for a very ugly, very badly behaved little boy. Just like a little boy, after the sugar rush comes the sudden crash. Lily leaves us alone for a while—perhaps there's something I want to say to Heathcote, she says. I look down at the weak old man. There's a lot I would have liked to say to him. That he hurt me. That his absence left a vacuum. But he's got me trapped again, with his vulnerability. So, I say nothing much—a few gentle lies. Heathcote's mask goes back on, his eyes close, and we leave.

The next day I arrive on the ward to find Heathcote's bed surrounded by nurses.

"He wants something, but we can't work out what it is," one of them tells me.

"Don't worry about it," I say. "It's probably just ice cream."

The nurses leave and I look down at Heathcote. After last night's escapades I feel like I know this man a lot better. I've seen him unmasked. We're even discovering that we have things in common. I love ice cream too.

"Is it ice cream you want?" I say loudly. "Mango ice cream? We'll have to ask the doctor to see if you're allowed any more."

Heathcote shakes his head, eyes desperate, and points to the noisy contraption forcing air into his lungs. He looks so utterly miserable, so beyond hope, that I can't work out why he's bothering to struggle on. In his situation I'm not sure if I'd want to. He looks up at me pleadingly and suddenly I'm struck by an awful thought. Is he trying to ask me to take the mask away so he can finally die?

I'm not sure if I give voice to this thought or if the idea just shows in my face. Either way, Heathcote's eyes widen in horror and he jabs at his emergency alarm button.

Nobody comes. It's the weekend and the hospital is overstretched, and in any case, thanks to me the nurses now think he's just a time-wasting ice-cream junkie. I give him a once-over myself. Nothing appears to be bleeping or seeping. He's making a fuss over nothing, I decide. Heathcote's hand drops the emergency alarm and crawls like an injured crab across his bed until it settles on a pen and paper.

"MASK LEAKING," he scrawls angrily.

When a nurse finally comes to inspect the mask, he finds there's nothing wrong with it at all. It's Heathcote's lungs that aren't working.

That is the last time I see Heathcote alive. He has a few more ups and downs, a few more flickers of false hope. Lily tells me he's finally started eating again, or at least that he's swallowed down a spoonful of porridge, and I make plans to bring him a flask of my grandmother's special rice porridge. It always does the trick when I'm ill. If I can just get him the right food, then perhaps he can recover from this for a year or a few months, at least. The next day, on Yana's birthday, Lily calls again. Heathcote is dead.

Chapter 33

Outside the kitchen window, a small pale spider performs a rope dance in a beam of morning light. Holding its delicate limbs elegantly in the air, it resembles an eight-pointed Chinese character spinning on a glowing thread. Aided by invisible pulleys, it glides smoothly up toward a lichen-covered branch where, unseen for now, the magpie sits waiting. Benzene holds still as a snake as the spider pirouettes into range and then, with a single sharp snap of applause, she ends the dance, crushing the spider's thorax and mangling its legs.

I blink and stare at the bird in a vacant sort of way as she celebrates her triumph over the spider with a dance of her own, slashing at the air with her beak and flicking victory with her tail. I feel almost totally blank. It's two weeks since Heathcote died and all I've been able to summon up is the emotional equivalent of white noise. Considering how much time I spend dreading catastrophe, it seems odd to flatline like this when one actually comes along. Perhaps Heathcote just wasn't a big enough part of my daily life to miss. I'd certainly notice this bird being gone more than I do him.

Other people seem to expect me to be totally catatonic. Friends have been sending kind messages offering to cook, or take care of the cleaning, or perform any other duties I might suddenly find myself incapable of; very tempting, but I'd feel like a con artist suckering people with counterfeit grief if I took any of them up on it. "Thanks," I reply, "but I barely knew the man, so I'm not exactly bawling my eyes out." The sadness of this statement has only occasionally broken through. I've tried to use music to make myself grieve in the right sort of way. I found out that Heathcote loved the Kinks, so I spent much of an afternoon listening to "Death of a Clown" on repeat until tears came, but even that felt hollow. I could make myself cry by listening to that song if it were a dog that had just died; there's nothing about it that's particular to Heathcote. If anything, I'm slightly suspicious of his death. The timing is uncanny. He dies the same day we had chosen to start trying for a child, as if his soul might be playing a game of inter-generational stepping stones.

Out on her branch, the bird scratches herself furiously and tiny feathers, gray and downy, fall from her nape and sink slowly to the ground. Next she picks and pecks at her tail, chipping away at the waxy tubes from which new purple-shining feathers emerge like amethyst from a cave wall. Shedding the old seems to be at once more painful and far simpler for her than it is for me. I wish I could just scratch off this smothering blankness I feel. I worry about not having the appropriate feelings, but I'm not even sure what the appropriate feelings might be in this situation. How do you let go of someone you never had? What I've lost isn't a person—I've hardly spent twenty hours with him in the last twenty years—but the hope of knowing a person. Perhaps the funeral tomorrow will make things clearer.

Later in the day Yana and I drive to Oxford in a car laden with swathes of fabric and bunches of flowers. Heathcote is having a

DIY funeral and somewhere along the way Yana got roped into helping make it look nice. Over the last fortnight, China and Lily have gone out of their way to include me in all the decisions about the funeral. At late-night meetings in their family friend's basement studio in West London I've found myself being called on to help make all sorts of choices for Heathcote: what type of coffin he'd like to lie in, what music he'd like, how he'd like his body to be disposed of. It turns out the only thing that was stopping me from being a part of Heathcote's life was him being alive. Now that he's dead I'm deeply enmeshed in his affairs—and am quite lost. When China turns to me and asks, What do *you* think he would have wanted? I can't work out if she's being deliberately cruel, or trying to be kind, or if she's simply as clueless as I am—or even if on some level she thinks I possess some sort of innate knowledge. If it were entirely up to me, I'd bake Heathcote into loaves of bread and feed him to the birds in the park. Or just burn the bastard and be rid of him.

I can't imagine who all these preparations are for. Surely Heathcote was a friendless hermit, too obsessed with his poetry to bother much with people? China and Lily seem to think otherwise. They've printed hundreds of funeral programs and bought an orchard's worth of apple saplings to line the aisle of the huge church they've booked for the ceremony, with the idea that people will take them home afterward and plant trees in memory of Heathcote. At their behest I've got an industrial-sized hot water urn in the trunk of the car for the mammoth cream tea China and Lily are laying out at the wake.

When we arrive at the wake venue, a charmingly decrepit event space near the church, to help set it up for tomorrow, we find China and Lily already hard at work lugging tables and putting out chairs. It makes me sad to see them doing all of this; doing more for Heathcote's corpse than he probably ever did for them while he was alive. I can't work out why they're bothering. Or why I am, for that matter, although I feel compelled to. It's certainly not because of anything I owe to Heathcote that I start unloading the car and fussing over the arrangement of the remembrance display; quite the opposite, in fact. This is something he owes me.

It's early evening by the time we start to make our way over to Heathcote's house for a small funeral-eve gathering. The place is almost exactly as I remember it from my last visit eight years ago. Hollyhocks sway tall outside the front door. Heathcote's oil paintings hem you in as you walk down the corridor. But someone has cleaned the place up. There's no cat food on the floor this time and no swarms of flies either, despite the dead body. Heathcote's picnic basket of a coffin lies on a table in the cozy, book-lined living room, its wicker lid buckled shut with leather straps. Next to the coffin is a makeshift coffee-table altar, with tealights illuminating framed pictures of Heathcote. Heathcote as a cherub-faced young boy. Heathcote thumbing his nose at the camera. Heathcote holding court at an Arthurian round table with a jackdaw by his side.

It's a select circle: a few locals, a few friends of China and Lily's mother making small talk over the top of the coffin. The man from the corner shop pops in to pay his respects. The mailman comes by too, and fondly recalls the hours he used to spend chatting with Heathcote. A young woman who grew up a few doors down tells me about how kind Heathcote was, how generous he was with his time, how he was, in fact, just like a father to her. I hear for the first time about Heathcote's open-door policy: His front door was literally always unlocked and open to anyone who wanted to stop by, which explains why, when I came to visit seven years ago, it swung open at my touch. I get a lump in my throat.

In the garden I smoke pot with someone whose name I immediately forget and down a few glasses of wine.

When nobody's looking, I go back into the living room and lift the lid of the coffin. Heathcote resembles a waxwork that's been left lying in the sun. I extend my index finger and give his forehead a slow prod. The cold skin slides over his skull like octopus flesh. I feel nothing but disappointment at my own lack of feeling.

I had a plan to take one of Heathcote's fingers; or perhaps it wasn't a plan, just a sick fantasy, but if that's true then it was quite a detailed one. The pruning shears are waiting in my bag. A psychoanalyst might point out the obvious Oedipal connotations of this, and they'd probably be right to do so. I wanted his finger as an object of power, a relic of sorts, a small part of Heathcote that could be mine and mine alone. China has already snipped off a lock of his hair for what are, I imagine, similar reasons. But now, face-to-face with the corpse, I find that the impulse has left me. Not because of any particular squeamishness on my part. It's just that the power this body once contained seems to have all leaked away. China and Lily's mother, Diana, enters the room and I quickly and guiltily pull down the lid of the coffin. I was worried about meeting her after our cold phone conversations so many years ago but, since then, dementia has stolen her away. She gives me a childlike smile and tells me how lovely everything is, and then breezes into the kitchen.

The framed image of the jackdaw flickering in the candlelight catches my eye. The bird is less of a mystery now—or at least it's become a small part of a greater mystery. Clearly Heathcote was more than able to care for many things and many people: for the elephants, for dolphins, for the mailman, for the little girl up the road, for the children of friends, for the chickens he kept in the garden and allowed to perch on his head, for the mangy street cat who took full advantage of his open-door policy. It was only with his own children—or at least with his own son—that his ability to exhibit care came unstuck. He could be *like* a father, but he struggled when it came to actually *being* a father.

The jackdaw winks at me again. It has been badly captured by the camera, smoky and out of focus. Perched inside its frame next to the coffin it brings to mind the odd spectacle of corvid funerals. Magpies and jackdaws both appear to do exactly what I am doing right now as I stand beside Heathcote's body. They have been observed holding funerals for their dead, or at least conducting death rituals of some kind: raucous gatherings whose exact purpose—an expression of grief, or anger, or an attempt to learn from the misfortunes of others—is unclear. They congregate alongside the bodies of their dead and examine them closely, noisily calling others to come and do the same. More sentimental observers have claimed that the birds are mourning, and that their cries suggest emotional pain. My time with a magpie has taught me that these birds are capable of great emotional complexity. But they are also practical creatures. The interpretation that makes most sense to me has it that they are interrogating their dead, carrying out a sort of group postmortem to ascertain what killed their comrade in the hope that this knowledge will allow them to avoid the same fate.

When I open the coffin lid again I search Heathcote's cadaver for a similar lesson. What went wrong in this man's life? And how can I stop myself from repeating his mistakes? The only lesson I can read from his ruined body is a caution against being an alcoholic and a heavy smoker who refused to do any exercise. There are posters up on the walls in my local GP's practice that tell me all that. Whatever it is I'm looking for, this corpse can't provide.

I shut the lid again and go up the narrow wooden stairs, opening the first door I come across, which, as luck would have it, happens to be Heathcote's study. In front of me is a dark wooden desk with a green leather top. A single bed is pressed up against the wall and there are disposable cardboard potties scattered around in conveniently placed piles. It looks to me like this was a room from which Heathcote very rarely emerged. I think back to the image of him at Port Eliot, filling vases and saucepans with piss, and wonder how a person can be so incapable of change. I turn to an enormous filing cabinet with hundreds of narrow drawers and start opening them at random. One contains half a dozen fake thumbs, hollow as the finger I wanted to steal. Another is full of magic coins. In one is a muddle of pictures of Heathcote and in another a cardboard box, in which I discover a modest collection of used condoms. I hesitate for a moment, then take one out and examine it, trying to determine whether it has been recently occupied, although I am unsure what the prophylactic equivalent of a cigarette smoking in an ashtray or a cinder still glowing in a fireplace might be. I stretch out the old latex and the contents flake. I have no idea what this means. I think about his loyal partner downstairs: here, but not really here. My mind goes in other directions. I cast my thoughts back to his last few public appearances. There was a woman, only a few years older than me, who often seemed to be by his side and whose absence now seems conspicuous. Maybe he really was a bastard until the end. Or maybe he just liked to masturbate into a Durex. The more I discover, the more of a stranger he seems.

I put the condom back with its friends and turn to Heathcote's desk. His laptop is there, but I don't touch it. It would make it too obvious, reveal why I'm really here too starkly, if I opened it and searched for my own name. I turn my attention to a plastic basket containing his personal effects from the hospital instead. A few notebooks, a few loose scraps of paper with jotted messages in an increasingly illegible hand. Nothing strikes me, except for one phrase that pops up several times in both English and Welsh: *Y Gwir Yn Erbyn Y Byd. The Truth Against the World.* The motto of the Druids, according to Heathcote. He told me that his father had taught him the phrase, which still seems strange to me. I struggle to imagine that miserable judge having had any druidic connections or magical tendencies. I trace Heathcote's calligraphy with my finger and wonder what it meant to him, wishing that I'd thought to ask. How can truth stand in opposition to the world? I think about Heathcote's stubborn refusal to admit he was dying, his deafness to the doctor's prognosis, his infuriating determination against all evidence that he would live to 120. Clearly truth meant something else to him. *The Truth Against the World.* The power of the word, the power of belief, the power of self-deception, as a weapon against reality. *Y Gwir Yn Erbyn Y Byd.*

I haven't been lurking at Heathcote's desk for long when someone appears at the door. It's the man I smoked pot with in the garden whose name I still can't recall. I scowl at him, trying to communicate that I'm having a moment and want to be left alone, but he comes in and sits down regardless. He's another one: another one to whom Heathcote was like a father, an older brother, a wise old man with infinite time. He tells me what a huge fan he was of Heathcote's work, how he heard about Heathcote's open-door policy and just turned up at the house one day, how honored—and slightly surprised—he was to be allowed to become a permanent fixture in Heathcote's life.

I can't help but resent this man, which is unfair of me because it's hardly his fault. In fact, thanks to him things are starting to make a bit more sense. Heathcote was happy to let this man, this unabashed admirer, in because it sounds like he was grateful for everything he got, that he would never have challenged Heathcote or made him feel bad. Like a stupid dog, I think, then catch myself. There's something in that hateful thought, though. Like an animal—like the jackdaw—this man was never going to ask any awkward questions. I get up and leave him alone with his grief. Everything feels the wrong way round.

The funeral the next day passes by in a sort of blur. We pull the coffin out through the living room window and parade it through the streets for a mile or so to the church. People swap in and out as they tire of carrying Heathcote's weight, but I refuse to let go, letting the coffin dig deep into my shoulder. In front of us someone bangs an enormous drum. Yana and my mum follow close behind. I worry for my mum. It's twenty-seven years since she last saw Heathcote and most of the people swarming around the coffin are no friends of ours. There have been moments over the years when Heathcote's badmouthing of my mum has reached even my ears, so his attacks on her must have been vociferous indeed. While watching out for my mum, I see the mob of mourners beginning to swell. I keep having to glance back over my aching shoulder, unable to believe that Heathcote had this many people in his life.

When we get to the church the size of the crowd hits me like a slap. The rows are packed. This man was no hermit. We set the coffin down in front of the altar as a piece of classical music plays over the PA, and then Heathcote's sonorous voice booms from above, filling the church. Heathcote describes the planet as seen from on high, from a heavenly perspective, godlike. "From space the planet is blue . . ." It's a recording I've heard before; the first few stanzas of *Whale Nation*, the poem he had just finished writing when he met my mother. His voice is so familiar, so alluring, so hypnotizing, and I feel a familiar longing rising up as the priest takes to the pulpit.

When the service ends I automatically trail after the coffin as it's picked up and carried out of the church, leaving everyone else standing in their rows. A hearse is waiting to return Heathcote's body to the mortuary. There are no immediate plans for the corpse. My sisters seem to have a block on the subject, so he's going back on ice. I stand in my toe-pinching leather shoes on the rough gravel, unsure what to do. I don't know how to be in this situation. Others emerge from the church. When they stop to talk, I find myself trying to pretend that I really knew Heathcote, telling a joke I found in one of his notebooks about the difference between a cat and a comma over and over again. (What's the difference between a cat and a comma? One has claws at the end of its paws, the other is a pause at the end of a clause.) "Isn't that so Heathcote?" I keep saying, until my mum taps me on the shoulder and pleads with me to stop.

At the wake, I don't know what to say to people, and people don't seem to know what to say to me. I try to encourage those who knew him to write more than "best wishes" in the book of remembrance. I want essays. Clear, detailed, intense memories. I'm still trying to find a way to take my piece of this man, to understand him. People seem confused. It reminds me of being a child and meeting people who said they knew my father. "Oh really," I'd reply brightly. "What's he like?" They would quickly back off, finding themselves in a more intense situation than they bargained for. I know from experience this is a futile exercise. This all feels very familiar. Hunting for Heathcote in the places he isn't. I leave Oxford feeling even more empty than when I arrived.

Chapter 34

After the funeral, I begin obsessively tracing and retracing my encounters with Heathcote. I see the dozens of missed opportunities, the openings I failed to spot, the overtures he made that I willfully ignored. I berate myself for not having tried harder. I should have tried to call more. I should have just turned up at his house. He had an open-door policy, after all. An open-door policy that everyone knew about—everyone except me. I was the one he couldn't be around. If, after Heathcote's death, feelings eluded me, they've all come knocking now. His final vanishing act has thrown me backward. I keep thinking about the helpless look in his eyes as I told him about cremation, his gory explosion when I turned up by his bedside, the letter I wrote him in blood, and memories happily suppressed come spurting up, too. The time, approaching psychosis, when I wished him dead, and believed my wish had the power to come true. A feeling of terrible responsibility consumes me. *I did it. My fault.*

I didn't think grief would be like this: a never-ending trial, with myself acting as prosecutor, judge, and hapless defendant all at once. But that's how it plays out. I go hunting for evidence to explain Heathcote's absences, and it's not hard to find. All the terrible things I've done in my life, real and imagined, come crowding into my head, from birth to present day. It's like having a mob of scolding crows flapping noisily around in there. They strike whenever they feel like it, no respect for time or place. At night when I'm trying to sleep I suddenly curl up in agony like I've been poisoned; on the top deck of the bus I beat myself around the head; hunched at a table in the café at the end of our street I start clawing at my face and rocking back and forth in my chair; while doing the dishes I hurl abuse at myself, forgetting there are other people in the house. "You stupid fucking cunt," I yell at a dirty saucepan as the memory of wetting myself in kindergarten spreads like a stain across the inside of my skull. I feel like an ant under a magnifying glass—but as well as being the ant I am also the boy aiming the fire. I plunge my fists into inanimate objects until the skin breaks and blood drips down my fingers. At times I feel like I'm a heartbeat away from seriously hurting myself or, worse, someone else.

Sometimes the awareness that Heathcote was at least partly to blame breaks through. At the supermarket, in the fruit aisle, I spot a packet of red grapes and feel a flash of anger at the memory of his tragic belief that red grapes could cure his incurable condition. "You stupid old man," I shout at the grapes, kicking at the fruit stand. A frail-looking gentleman shuffling down the aisle toward me stops in his tracks and edges nervously away. I add scaring vulnerable retirees to my list of crimes.

These feelings, though unusual in their severity, are also very familiar, and I reach for familiar solutions. I drink too much, smoke too much cannabis, overdo it with codeine and sleeping pills, and this creates its own ecosystem of regret. My paranoia—hardly a placid beast under normal circumstances—grows wings.

Yana tries to help, or at least tries to get me to talk about what's going on, but I seal myself off from her, both physically and emotionally. And if discussing parenthood was difficult before, it's now become completely impossible. I spend more time than ever shut away with the bird. With Benzene on my wrist, thought escapes me. I lose my sense of loss in the blackness of her eyes. The vengeful voice inside my head is hushed by the beat of her wings, if only for a while. She prods the open wounds on my knuckles with her beak and samples the residue with her thin black tongue. *Food*, she thinks. Maybe there's something I can learn from her unsentimental attitude. After all, what's death—or a dead body—to a magpie but an opportunity to grow?

The more time I spend with the bird, the more I begin to wonder if she might have the power to lift me permanently out of the trap I've thrown myself into. I remember reading Helen Macdonald's *H Is for Hawk*, a book by an academic who, in the wake of her father's sudden death, trained a peregrine falcon to fly from her wrist. I seem to recall that the bird's killing weight on her arm helped her somehow; took her out of herself. I think back to the magpie's days on the farm, remember the thrill of her flying away and the even greater thrill as she soared back. A bird that always returns could be an antidote to loss. It makes perfect sense, in a dream-logic sort of way.

A magpie is no falcon, of course. But a professional animal trainer I've befriended—a rather odd man who lives with a pair of crows—has told me that it's possible to train a magpie to have perfect recall using falconry techniques. He did so a few years ago for a jewelry commercial, and I've seen further evidence online. A while back, he sent me instructions and links to all the equipment I would need. Now, I decide, the time has come to give it a go. Benzene's new flight feathers are just asking to play against the sky; and I have an urge to escape myself. I imagine my fantasy finally coming true—of being able to stretch out my arm in the park and a bird appearing like magic on the end of it; of sending her flying back up over the trees and part of me soaring away with her. On the farm she's always come back—although only in her own sweet time. Flying her in the city comes with a few more risks—eight million of them, and growing by the day—but the rewards, I am certain, will be even greater.

When Benzene sees the falconry equipment—the leather anklets, the long spool of nylon string, the metal clip, and the little leather leash—she immediately takes off to her highest branch. This is not unexpected. She fears the new, and any novel object, such as a toy or perch, is always initially treated with suspicion. This is fine. I have patience, and I have worms. Every day for a week I spend a little time trying to familiarize her with the leather anklets, letting her nibble and play with them. I create positive associations with them by giving her plenty of live treats. The first step is fitting the anklets. Then I'll fly her on the end of a string, like a kite; and once she's proven that she always comes back, I'll do away with the string and fly her free. With a little training, a little love, she'll come whenever I call. Then she can accompany me wherever I go; a constant companion. A bird on the head keeping thoughts at bay.

Benzene is happy about the extra worms and the attention; and she always enjoys chewing on a bit of leather. But if I so much as think about fitting the anklets around her legs, she shoots out of reach. If I persist, she begins flying back and forth from one end of the aviary to the other, springing off the wire so frantically it starts to feel like she's bouncing around the inside of my skull.

Eventually I snap. Early one morning I catch her in my hands and, ignoring her angry shouts and snapping beak, I fix the anklets in place. The animal trainer told me I might have to resort to this.

"She'll thank you once she understands what they're for," he reassured me. But Benzene never gives me the chance to show her what they're for. She stops talking to me, won't even come near me, no matter how many worms I wave at her from beneath her branch. It's as if, with a single act of betrayal, I've severed the bond between us.

She spends days obsessively tugging at the leather thongs around her matchstick legs, and then just sitting, worn out and depressed, on her branch. After a week of this, she comes and finds me at my desk and sits on my wrist. She looks up at me in silence and simply stares. It's like being locked in a no-blinking competition with your own guilty conscience. I feel terrible; here's yet another bad thing I've done. I catch her gently in my hands. This time there are no angry squawks as, using a pair of nail scissors, I carefully cut her free. The bird nibbles her shins, quacks like a duck, and flaps off, leaving me even more miserable than before. I can't fly my way out of this or punch my way through it. I'm stuck in a trap of my own making.

NEST

Chapter 35

I stretch out my arm in the park and a bird materializes on my wrist, an acid-green parakeet with needle-sharp talons and kaleidoscope eyes. In the sweet chestnut trees around me, dozens more of these strange, out-of-place birds watch, clicking their tongues inside their rosehip beaks. Two more swoop down and fight for room on my forearm, leaving tiny puncture wounds in my flesh as they squabble over the mound of peanuts in my palm. Beside me, China and her children stand with arms outstretched. Soon they too are lousy with parakeets. The boys squeal with shock and delight as the exotic birds stitch their way across the soft fish belly of their arms.

All around us, strangers do the same. An olive-skinned old man with a backpack full to the brim with sunflower seeds pulls parakeets from the air like a magician conjuring silk handkerchiefs and passes them out as if they were cotton candy; a solitary woman shrieks unselfconsciously, lost in her own private joy as no less than six birds bash beaks across her shoulders; a veiled woman's eyes shine as a parakeet struts along the armrest of her wheelchair.

A hundred years ago, the ancestors of these Indian ring-necked parakeets escaped their cages and somehow flourished in London's microclimate, despite being half a world away from their natural habitat. Now they fly in flocks hundreds strong over the capital, bringing delight, confusion, concern, and a lot of noise wherever they settle. For some reason, here—and, as far as I know, only here—around this one particular row of sweet chestnut trees in Hyde Park, these feral birds know no fear. It's like a little corner of Eden, but with more selfie sticks. The birds have learned to accept humans, and the humans have learned to accept the birds: a taming that goes two ways. If only the same could be done with the magpie: It's the world that needs training if she's to fly free.

I decant my parakeets onto China, adding peanuts and sunflower seeds to her shoulders and her hair to encourage even more birds to descend from the trees. Soon she is lost beneath a rude mantle of screaming birds.

"Urgh," she says, half grinning and half grimacing as one of them squirts out a long, thin shit onto her hand. "Horrible vermin."

Her horror makes me smile, although for a moment I'm not sure why. Then I realize that doing this—inflicting these manky parrots on her—is the first time I've really felt myself inhabiting the role of little brother. After Heathcote's death, I had wondered what would happen to the bond between us, wondered whether it would dissolve once the emergency that bound us together had passed. But those fears seem to have been unfounded. It's three months since his death; we are into autumn now. The boys have filled their pockets with horse chestnuts, and ours too, and the scythe of the seasons is steadily cutting off the leaves of the trees around us. Heathcote's body has been brought out of the deep freeze and burned: blood boiled, DNA unwound, the charred fragments tipped into a giant coffee grinder and whizzed to dust. And here we all are. This continuation feels like it might be a small act of rebellion; a sign that the skeleton grip of the almighty father is crumbling.

Of course, our continuing unity might just be a sign that the emergency isn't yet over. China, despite her wavering smile, seems haunted by the ghost of regret. At times she seems convinced that everything is all her fault, which sounds awfully familiar. The shadow play flickering across the walls of my skull is no less frightening. I've been spending more time than ever lost in an alternative universe in which the police are always waiting outside my door; every phone call threatens to bring news that I have gone insane and done something awful; every knock at the door is someone coming to kill me. This relentless, tedious, repetitive psychodrama is affecting Yana's life too. Trying for a child is supposed to be a joyous thing and she wants to talk about the future. But all I can do is silently rake over the coals of the past and in them see the seeds of the inferno to come—leaving her utterly alone in her optimism and excitement.

Looking around us at the strangers with their sacks of seed, I wonder what is missing from their lives. I sometimes feel that you can guess the weight of a person's troubles by the size of the bread bag they bring for the birds. Feeding the birds is a pleasure at once simple and complex. It's a way for people who feel bad to do something unambiguously good; a way for people who feel like they lack power or control to exert some small influence over the world; a way to fill a hole. Interacting with animals is good for us: It's been shown to lower the heart rate, reduce stress levels, and boost oxytocin, the love hormone. There's a line in Heathcote's jackdaw poem where he quotes Emily Dickinson on birds: "I hope you love birds too. It is economical. It saves going to heaven." Birds are medicine.

Our parakeets efficiently hull the sunflower seeds we offer

them and mash the peanuts with their pincer-like beaks. One of the boys tries to pet one and is rewarded with a sharp nip. The birds stay with us only as long as we make it worth their while. As soon as the food runs out, they're off, back into the trees, leaving us holding handfuls of empty husks.

Halfway up the furrowed trunk of an oak, I spot a jackdaw spying on us through a single gemstone eye. I point it out to China and she gives me a funny look. I dip my hand into my rucksack, fish out the last few peanuts, and advance slowly toward the tree. I feel certain I can summon this bird down too. I can bring the wild to hand, tame the untamable. The jackdaw landing on me would be like a blessing, like absolution. A tonic for the soul. Something that might set me free from this weight of responsibility. The jackdaw, tucked away almost invisibly in the shadow of a bough, realizes it's been seen and tenses up. It wants no part of this. I drop my gaze and slow my pace, holding my offering of peanuts up blindly to the oak. When I look again, the bird's black wings are carving the air, slicing through empty space into nothing.

I come back inexplicably crestfallen and together we make our way to the park exit. China and I walk in step for a while, not saying anything. She frowns at the ground, kneading a thought with her brows. Eventually she tells me that she's thinking of going back to Port Eliot, the estate in Cornwall where Heathcote lived for a decade. Where he had the jackdaw. Where he and my mum lived with me. It seems he never bothered to move out when he left, so there are still rooms full of all his things. Maybe letters. Maybe diaries. Maybe more about the jackdaw than is contained in that poem; maybe more about his inner world than he's ever confessed to me.

"If I go," China says, "would you like to come with me?"

Chapter 36

The deciduous trees drop their leaves and sprout new shoots, the jackdaws and magpies bury their winter pantries and dig them up again, and the first spring flowers have stirred and bloomed by the time China and I get around to boarding a train south to Cornwall. I haven't been to Port Eliot since I was a baby, and although I have no true memories of that period, no conscious ones at least, I nevertheless feel like I'm heading toward familiar territory, a world built from stories. The landscape passes in a wet green blur and I get the strangest sense that time is unzipping as we race over the tracks, and that soon I'll be able to step right through and finally see things as they really were. The cottage in the woods with its walnut trees and well; the lord of the manor with a face like a carelessly carved joint of beef; the pheasants that rained down from the sky and were mashed into baby food; the night in spring when Heathcote disappeared.

Opposite me, China is prodding an anemic egg and cress sandwich. Her lips are pressed tight, the corners turned down. For her the past is no fantasy. From the snippets she's let slip, it doesn't sound like Port Eliot was an especially happy place for her. Heathcote more or less abandoned her and Lily and their mum to go and live there; allegedly so he could focus on his writing. With that in mind, him suddenly starting up a new family in Port Eliot with my mum must have come as a shock and an insult.

"It's not like he would have changed if he'd lived, you know," China says, continuing a conversation we were having a few miles back. We've both been picking at the past like children with scabs, constantly worrying the wound so it never has a chance to heal. I've been thinking a lot about my encounters with Heathcote at the hospital, which, imperfect though they were, represented a reconciliation of sorts. Had he survived, then maybe I'd be asking him for answers to the questions that are knocking around inside my head, instead of having to go chasing jackdaws and dusty relics. Or maybe not. I suspect China is probably right. Cherries and sympathy aren't enough to break the habit of a lifetime.

By the time our train arrives at its destination, the sun has started shining, and on the walk to Port Eliot primroses and daffodils beam out at us from the grassy verges of the village lane. China leads the way down a winding path that carries us into the stone-cold shade of an imposing chapel, double-towered and ancient, its deep-set door surrounded by tiers of carved chevrons like rows of teeth in an enormous mouth. China skirts around it, heading for a gap in the thick yew hedge that encircles the churchyard. She hops nimbly over a locked wrought iron gate and I follow, landing back in the light.

The stately home of Port Eliot crouches over the landscape like an enormous lazy toad; a long, squat, sandy-colored toad with crenulations running like ridges along its back and a rounded tower for a head. In the valley beneath it, the River Tamar splays into mudflats, and the famous railway bridge totters on spindly legs through the air.

A German shepherd standing at attention outside the gatehouse tracks us silently with its eyes as we make our way down the slope toward the house. I have no idea what sort of welcome we're in for. Heathcote's friend Peregrine, the previous Lord Eliot, is dead, and his successor is a teenage boy. There are some rumors of a family rift and, according to China, there is a chance we will have to be accompanied around the estate by a security guard to make sure we don't take anything that isn't ours.

We walk cautiously past the dog through an open set of double doors and into an enclosed courtyard. One of the caretakers comes out to greet us, a gangling former soldier who, perhaps out of professional habit, gives us a quick situation report. Most of the house, he tells us, is sealed shut because of asbestos and mold—and because things keep going missing.

"It's like *Game of Thrones* around here," he mutters. "Poison and politics."

All Heathcote's things are stashed somewhere called the Knife Room, he explains, down in the underbelly of the house. We follow him back outside to the courtyard where, behind an asbestos decontamination tent, a well-worn wooden door is set into the base of the house. He gives it a bash and tug, not bothering with a key, and the door creaks open, releasing a blast of cold, damp air.

Behind the door is a tunnel that seems to run the length of the house. Murky light wells illuminate it only so far, then it vanishes in shadow. Somewhere in the dark guts of the house, a bell softly tinkles, and out of the abyss a black-and-white cat comes casually sauntering to rub itself against my ankles.

Lighting the way with our phones, we advance along a white plastic carpet laid along the middle of the tunnel by the decontamination workers. Where natural light and water have poured in from above, algae wetly blooms on the surface of the stone walls around us. Discarded objects line our route. A rusty iron cog. A child's bicycle. A boiler lying on its side like an unexploded bomb. We lurch to the left and I stumble over a pipe. I have a memory of someone telling me that Peregrine hated the sight of children so much that he used to insist that they use the tunnels under the house rather than share the corridors with him. I wonder if it's true, and if it is, I wonder why Heathcote—a man with three children—chose to live here for so long. I bash my shins against a shadowy object and hope at least that the tunnels were better lit back then.

Eventually we come to a halt. The caretaker fumbles for a switch and a pale bulb reveals the Knife Room to be a dank chamber about the size of a shipping container. Beside me, a rusty ax is sunk deep into a log and the floor is carpeted with damp wood chippings. Three of the walls are almost entirely obscured by stacks of cardboard boxes, all of them Heathcote's. Water has dripped down from the ceiling and along one of the walls and from it a purple and yellow mold has spread, crumbling everything in its path. China gingerly lifts the flap of one of the affected boxes and eases out a bundle of letters. They turn to mush in her hands.

"If there were any lost masterpieces in there," she says, "they're lost forever now."

She seems relieved that a third of our burden has been eaten. We look at the surviving boxes stacked against the other two walls. Their labels, written by a long-dead housekeeper, hint at the mess Heathcote left behind when he finally gave up his rooms here. A box marked ROUND ROOM, TOP OF WARDROBE contains hundreds of pages of handwritten notes, yellowed newspaper clippings, and reams of fan mail. LEFT HAND WINDOWSILL is full of rotting books, cassette tapes, and loose scraps of paper. Another box, marked FLOOR, is stuffed with trousers. It's as if he upped and left his friend Peregrine as suddenly as he left my mum and me. I don't actually know how long he stayed on here after he had his breakdown and cut himself off from us; perhaps all this disorder speaks of a mind that was still in ruins. Or perhaps he was just a slob.

I start pulling things out of boxes at random: a play sent to Heathcote by Harold Pinter; legal letters relating to his failure to pay my mum child support; sheaves and sheaves of correspondence with a society for whale enthusiasts; a broken plastic thumb that he would have once used to make silk handkerchiefs and lit cigarettes vanish before people's eyes; and a slide image only slightly larger than a postage stamp that, when I hold it up to the light, shows my mum in miniature juggling in a field, silver balls suspended midflight and a grin frozen on her face. Deeper in the box, I find what must be the husks of those very same juggling balls, their leather dry and cracked, empty of stuffing. I look at the picture of my mum again. Her whole world is just about to come tumbling down around her.

"Let's come back to all this later," China says. "I'll show you around."

Back outside, she points out the maze, the ornamental pool, the botanical gardens as we stroll through the grounds. We stop and sit on a bench set in the shade of a rhododendron and admire the view. The green valley is flecked with black dots, jackdaws and rooks scattered like obsidian beads. Between them, the river slithers toward the horizon like a golden-brown basilisk.

There are still traces of Heathcote to be found in the fabric of this place. China juts her chin up toward a curving set of windows on the second floor of a rounded tower.

"That's where Dad was," she says.

To me it looks like the best spot in the house, with almost

panoramic views of the grounds and beyond. It must have been like living in an incredibly grand crow's nest. Not a bad place to raise a jackdaw, either. I imagine him looking out from the tower with his bird on his shoulder, streaks of white covering his jacket, then unclasping the window and watching his sprite fly away, seeing the world through the bird's blue eyes.

At the base of the tower is one of Heathcote's carvings, a demonic-looking creature in a cowl whose features have been cut, life-size, from the rooted trunk of a tree. I stand in front of the figure, who is only slightly shorter than me, and run my finger along the deep gouges that form the folds in his robes. It's Dando, China explains, a sinful local monk who was, according to legend, dragged to hell by the devil himself after foolishly accepting a drink on the Sabbath. Lichen creeps over the monk's weather-worn, slightly feminine face like a skin condition. It's not clear if he's supposed to be laughing or screaming.

Of course, Heathcote didn't live in the tower for all of his time here. Perhaps it was because of Peregrine's reputed aversion to children that Heathcote was given the use of the old pig farmer's cottage for when his came to stay, and when it looked like he was going to have a family here full-time, he moved there permanently. Or at least that was the idea.

It's to this cottage that China proposes we go now. I've never seen a picture of it, but I've imagined it often: a sort of gingerbread house in a woodland clearing, with a thatched roof, glowing windows, and a smoking chimney.

"It's not a very nice place," China says as we walk away from the big house. "It was always so cold and dark when I was there."

We pass a fishing lake, where two fat anglers cast lines in the sun, then enter a wood full of mossy oaks and strangling vines. The floor is a sea of wild garlic: thick bunches of wavering green leaves that surround spear-like shoots, with pointed buds on the cusp of bursting into delicate white flowers. China and I both stoop to tear off a few fragments and put them in our mouths. The bluebells haven't quite come in yet but they are close. It would have been around this time of year that Heathcote had his breakdown.

China was right. The closer we get to the cottage, the darker and colder it becomes as the forest closes in on us. The path slips from gravel to bare mulch and the wild garlic dies away. The cottage itself is underwhelming: a short, boxy building constructed from slabs of gray stone set in the ruins of a pig farm. Somewhere nearby a water main has burst and the half-collapsed barns in front of the cottage teeter over a pool of stagnant water. It's far from the cozy nest I'd imagined.

I knock on the door and a paunchy, middle-aged man with pale skin and a steel-gray buzz cut answers. I explain that I used to live here and although he doesn't seem especially keen to let me look around, he's too polite to actually say no, so I step inside.

Over the threshold it's actually quite cheerful. I pass through a dining room with a rustic wooden table, cast-iron stove, and a trinket-jumbled wooden dresser. The cottage is built into a shallow hill, so toward the kitchen it sinks below ground level. Through the window the forest floor is in line with my eyes, a lattice of ivy and dead branches. A couple of blackbirds barrel past, squabbling noisily over which of them has the right to call this patch home. I feel like a rabbit peeping out from its burrow.

I have a more realistic picture now of how we all lived, but I struggle to find any clues embedded in the cottage that might explain why it all fell apart. I suppose caring for a newborn through the winter in this isolated environment might have been tough. But if so, spring should have brought hope. I imagine Heathcote stepping out every day to find himself in the middle of this forest, green shoots in the undergrowth, mist rising from the valley, birdsong breaking the dawn. For a happy person, it would have been heaven. But not for Heathcote. The year's new leaves unfurled and his mind unraveled.

As we walk back along the woodland path, I think about my mum's account of the days that followed Heathcote's disappearance, how she walked the mile or so to the house with me in her arms only to be met with Lord Eliot's spiteful rebuff. As we get closer the crenulations rise from the grass, then the sheer walls and thick wooden doors—an obscene defense to use against a mother with a baby in her arms.

When we arrive back at the house, Peregrine's younger son, Louis, a man in his forties with unkempt brown hair and kind eyes, offers to give us a quick tour of Heathcote's old wing. He seems slightly crestfallen when we accept his offer, nervous even about entering his own childhood home, and I wonder what drama is playing out in his family.

Louis leads us up a staircase, through a padded green door, down a narrow passageway, and through a side door into the main entrance hall where dusty portraits of people who must be Eliots through the ages glare down at us from the walls. Above our heads a black chandelier hangs from a thick chain and by the heavy double doors sabers and flintlock rifles rest on their stands. Everything seems tired and broken, like the house's heart is no longer quite in it and it's quietly trying to seep back down into the soil. The once-sumptuous red carpet that lines the grand staircase has been worn to rags. Expensive silk wallpaper hangs, torn, from the walls, revealing blooms of black mold on the plaster beneath. In some places, actual mushrooms are growing from the walls. With Louis as our guide, we advance down the dark, musty corridors toward Heathcote's old chambers.

After a few days of trying and failing, my mum managed to sneak into these corridors too, entering the house through the servants' quarters. I've no doubt she must have been furious with Heathcote for leaving her and their baby alone in the woods without so much as a note of explanation. She must have been frightened as well, and desperate to try to help the man she loved, and who she thought loved her too. Over the years, I've questioned her closely in an effort to understand what went wrong in Heathcote's head. There must have been some early warning signs. Surely people don't go insane overnight. But that's exactly what seems to have happened. One day it was bluebells and bliss, the next Heathcote was thin air.

On the first floor, we walk down an uneven wooden corridor toward the rounded tower at the end, toward the room where my mum finally found Heathcote mad-eyed and gibbering.

Unlike much else on this ghost ride, Heathcote's main room is similar to how I have always imagined it: a rounded, light-filled, luxurious space, with a marble fireplace and huge wood-framed windows, like a captain's quarters in a Spanish galleon. The Persian carpet is threadbare, and the pale olive-green paint is peeling from the walls, but somehow it seems to have resisted the rot that runs through the rest of the house.

After my mum and I were ejected, Heathcote fell back onto the pillow of his social privilege, a cushy version of care in the community for Old Etonians. Lord Eliot's housekeeper brought him his meals and he was finally free from his obligations. That's when he seems to have decided that he hadn't had a breakdown after all, that he'd ended things because of creative differences, because of that somber enemy of art, "the pram in the hall."

Apart from highlighting quite how easy it was for Heathcote to dispense with my mother and me, I don't know what I expected to find in this room. Heathcote lived here for over ten years; he wrote here, ate here, pissed here, raised a jackdaw here, and hid from the rest of his responsibilities here. But the only sign of him I can see now is a copy of one of his books—*Sacred Elephant*—that has been propped up on a dresser by a window. Did I really think the upholstery was going to start whispering to me? The answers I want are hardly going to leap out from the floorboards. Heathcote, if he's to be found at Port Eliot at all, is underground, packed into those damp boxes in the basement.

China and I spend the rest of the day wheeling Heathcote's junk out through the darkened passageway that runs under the house and loading it into the back of a Luton van. It's all being taken to a studio space in West London to be sorted and then hopefully sold. China grumbles something about how she's having to clear up her dad's mess yet again. We cover ourselves in the dust of undisturbed decades; rotten paper, mold, and mouse droppings graying us like ghosts. When the job's done, China and I say our goodbyes and I watch as she beats dirt from her clothes, then hauls herself up into the cab with the driver. As the van growls to life, I turn and head back up the hill toward the church.

Alone on the platform at the village train station, I find myself thinking not about Heathcote and what might have caused him to crack, but about my mum, and how she managed to find the strength to carry on afterward. Abandoned by the father of her child; sent packing by the lord of the manor; nowhere to go; it'd be enough to bring anyone down. But somehow, despite the extra gravity, she just about managed to keep all the balls up in the air. I think again about the slide picture I found in the basement of her juggling on the lawn in front of the big house. Heathcote taught her to do that during their courtship. He'd turn up at my mum's apartment and together they'd juggle for hours, first with a set of silver balls, then batons, then eventually flaming torches. He even carved her a sculpture of juggling balls from a knotty piece of wood, which she eventually gave to me, and which now sits on a shelf above my desk. After he left, and turned so nasty, you could imagine that some people might never want to juggle again, might never want to risk anything again. But faced with catastrophe, my mum found a way to pick the treasure out of the ashes. She still sometimes juggles fire to this day; paraffin-soaked torches that she sends arcing up into the night sky, flames roaring as they whirl, somehow never allowing herself to get burned.

A couple of jackdaws land on top of a lamppost on the other side of the tracks, interrupting my train of thought. They examine me closely for a while and then drop, one after the other, to the floor to dig out crumbs of food from between cracks in the paving slabs. Together they pick the platform clean, then hop down onto the tracks, never seeming to go more than a few meters from each other, obviously a breeding pair. If Heathcote's jackdaw survived, then I suppose one of these two could very well be family. A jackdaw sibling of sorts.

Neither of them shows any signs of recognizing me as they swagger importantly along the railway tracks, inspecting empty chip bags, bottle tops, fragments of Benson & Hedges cigarettes. Side by side in the sun, they look more metallic than the rusted brown track beneath their feet. Black steel and gunmetal gray. Their language is metallic too: The distinctive *tchack-tchack* call, from which jackdaws are said to have derived their name, is high and harsh and slightly eerie, like the singing of a frozen lake as the ice cracks in spring. Their utterances carry meaning. Let's go out. Let's go home. Danger. Food over here. I watch them for a little longer, then they take off in silent unison in that wordless way birds sometimes do, communicating their intent with a blink, a gesture, or a thought. I let my mind soar off with them for a moment, then return to earth. There's crow work to do down here; a dead man to dissect.

Chapter 37

I lie back in the bath and run my fingers through my hair. They snag on tangled locks, where fragments of meat and bird shit have cohered into stubborn clumps. I work these magpie gifts loose, ripping out much of the affected hair in the process, and then I allow myself to sink beneath the surface of the water. I listen to the sounds of the house; the plumbing; a deep hum; my blood thudding around in my head; and then a sharp rap, a *click-clack, click-clack* that drowns the other noises out. I resurface to find myself nose to beak with the magpie. Without waiting for permission, Benzene hops from the edge of the tub onto my knee, sidles down my thigh, and helps herself to my bath. She sploshes around on my chest, waist-deep, and gleefully shakes water into my face and up my nostrils, coating me with a thin film of bird grease. When I get out, she rubs herself dry on my towel.

As I dress, Benzene leaps up to the showerhead and shakes herself, body and tail. With a rattle of feathers she triples in size, like a puffer fish exploding in fright. Using her beak for a comb, she brushes her feathers one by one, putting them in their correct order. Once my shirt is on, she jumps down to my arm and gently wipes her cheeks on my sleeve.

I pack a few bits and pieces into a backpack. Today the unpicking begins. Heathcote's papers are all stacked and waiting on the other side of town. I worry about what I'm going to find there; and I worry about what I won't find. Is it even possible to know someone after they're dead? I think about the misshapen picture someone might create of me if the only thing they had to go on was the paper trail I've left behind so far: court documents, a few damning headlines, pages and pages of notes about birds. I can only hope Heathcote is less guarded on paper than he was in person.

Benzene whistles. She's parading in front of the mirror on the landing outside our room, gazing lovingly at her reflection. Every now and then she emits a shriek and a clatter as she performs leaps, pirouettes, and other acrobatic feats, admiring her own agility and the fine flash of her wing feathers with unabashed pride. I hold out my hand and she hops to it. I try to read her thoughts, but they're as elusive as mine must be to her. She nibbles my knuckles, quacks like a duck, and then, with a gentle turn of my wrist, I send her into flight.

Benzene is a bright star in the days that follow. An airy spirit who keeps me afloat as I submerge myself in the outpourings of Heathcote's mind. A deluge of thoughts, images, dreams, and memories springs from the damp, moldy boxes we brought back from Cornwall. The material is deeper, more revealing, and, in some places, far darker than I'd imagined—at times too dark to look at with ease. There are diaries. Letters. Obscene drawings. Designs for flying machines. Descriptions of suicide attempts. Ecstatic accounts of gay sex. More used condoms. Ravings from a stay in a mental asylum that are more unpleasant than anything I've ever read. Scrawls of despair and anger from the eye of the breakdown he had after my birth. And there are photographs too:

Heathcote as a little boy in a sunny garden, clutching an apple in his hands; Heathcote in his naked and beautiful twenties, on all fours, his penis hanging down like a long, thin udder; Heathcote, much older, stuffing banknotes into his anus. *You wanted me*, the boxes seem to say. *Well, here I am. Happy now?*

The Archive, as my sisters and I have taken to calling it, has now been amassed in the large studio space in West London to be sorted and prepared for sale. I have no financial stake in the sale—I wasn't mentioned in Heathcote's short will and didn't expect to be—but I'm all for auctioning the lot to the highest bidder, for my sisters' sakes. Why shouldn't they finally get something out of the old man? A little compensation, at least. They take a different line. They don't want Heathcote to go to the University of Texas, no matter how much money is on the table. They want him to be somewhere close, ideally in a London institution, so they can visit.

If Heathcote can be said to exist anywhere, now that his body has been burned, it's surely here, in this enormous hoard of words. They spill from boxes, overflow from garbage bags; not just the vanload from Port Eliot, but the contents of his study, and the cellar, and a storage unit, too. A coffee-stained, moldering impression of his life, as detailed and as delicate as the papery structure left behind by wasps after summer.

In the Archive, the sour smell of mold is somehow even more overpowering than it was at Port Eliot, as if the material is rebelling against the light. At the end of each day I come away filthy, sneezing, and feeling lousy—but I keep going back for more. I need this. My approach is far from methodical. I attack the body of words and images like a carrion bird, looking for the wound that will yield to my prying beak, the original injury that unravels the man. I peel back layers of skin, pick over the bones, snip my way to the heart of the matter. A patchwork biography begins to emerge; a rough story told in scavenged scraps. It feels almost like stealing, like robbing the grave, except it's not the treasures that interest me. Heathcote's glories hardly get a glance. It's the traumas I'm searching for. Answers to those same old questions. Why does a person disappear? What makes a man run from his child? Why was Heathcote so afraid of family? What forces guided that nocturnal flight in spring so many years ago?

The closest to the beginning I can get is the photo of the little boy standing on a sun-bleached lawn, holding what appears to be an apple in front of him with both hands. Heathcote looks about five, so it must be a year or two after the end of the Second World War. He's neatly dressed. Leather sandals buckled around white socks pulled above his ankles. Knobbly knees. Voluminous shorts fastened high above his waist. White short-sleeved shirt buttoned to the neck. It's not a formal picture, however. It's loving and intimate: a portrait of a boy at play in high summer. His mother—my grandmother—is surely the photographer. Heathcote writes elsewhere of her little Box Brownie, how she made him dance and smile for the sad goblin she claimed lived in the machine. A glimpse of Heathcote before the damage was done. Or is it? It's important to resist the temptation to read too much into a photograph, but it's hard not to think that he holds his apple a little nervously, smiles a little uncertainly. Heathcote's father appears in portraits too. An unsmiling, pig-eyed man in a judge's wig staring down the camera. Did he dish out beatings to this tiny child? If not at this tender age, then certainly later. Heathcote's younger sister, Prue, spends a few afternoons alongside me at the Archive, skirting around memories of their father's reign of terror.

"At least he never hit our mother," she says. "Although he did once throw a joint of mutton at her head."

It can't have been very long after the photo in the garden was taken that Heathcote was sent away to boarding school on his father's orders. Sending a child this young to a British boarding school seems, to me, like abuse by proxy. How old was he when discipline took the place of affection? Five? Six? A mummy's boy sent away to be made into a man. Corporal punishment. Institutional bullying. And perhaps even worse, too. Heathcote was small, defenseless. He seems to have coped by dreaming of escape, dreaming of flight. His jackdaw poem, although written much later, begins by recalling a fantasy he had around this age of having a jackdaw as a friend, a magical creature who would talk to him and protect him. The fantasy of a lonely and unprotected child. From Eton, he writes to Dunlop Rubber, requesting they send him a balloon large enough to carry him away. The reply from Dunlop Rubber is dated in June, which makes me wonder where exactly Heathcote was planning to escape from: school or home?

I next find him at Oxford, studying law just like his father wants him to. Perhaps there, for the first time in his life, he has space to breathe and to see what lies at the end of the path he's following: a nightmare vision of his own face imprisoned in his father's horsehair wig. He finally works up the courage to inflate his escape balloon. He writes a polite, cautious, perhaps even nervous letter to his father announcing that he intends to give up his studies, that he's going to become an artist and writer instead. The arguments that follow echo in Heathcote's ears all the way to his deathbed. *How can you be a writer when you don't know anything?*

I can't find a scrap in the Archive about any of this, but Prue shows me the long wooden ruler her father smashed over Heathcote's head when he came down from Oxford after that letter. I finger its jagged edge and think how odd it is for her to have kept it all these years. Evidence, I suppose. Proof that those things really did happen. I think again about the story Heathcote told my mum, about the time his father came into his room to beat sense into him, how Heathcote fought back for the first time in his life and his father had a minor heart attack. It's possible that in that moment he wished his father dead. Perhaps he even said as much as he shoved the man to the floor. Then, not long after, the fatal heart attack came. Heathcote's father died in the summer of 1964, and perhaps it was then that Heathcote's belief in his own terrible power was born.

After this, his dreams of escape and flight seem to take on a darker tone. More scraps of paper emerge. He tries to hang himself but is caught. On one undated sheet he writes about another attempt in great detail. He climbs onto the parapet of Charing Cross Bridge, makes his peace with God, and inches toward the edge. On the road behind him a man stops his car and climbs out. "Where is Charing Cross?" the man asks. "We're on Charing Cross Bridge," Heathcote says dismissively, not looking away from the river pulsing beneath him. The man carries on talking. His name is Barnes, he says. He lives in Camberwell. He tells Heathcote he's thinking of going home to fry up some bacon and eggs and invites him to come along. It takes a monumental effort for Heathcote to turn his head away from the drop, like revolving a mountain on its axis. When his eyes meet those of the stranger his will to die withers. He steps back from the edge.

Heathcote next appears in his family home. I follow him across the tightly lined A5 pages of a typewritten journal that tracks his early twenties, watching as he hunts the ghost of his father from room to room. In his parents' bedroom, he sees his father dressing and undressing, recalls his gnat-like legs, the burst capillaries spattered against the white flesh behind his knees, his red, rashed neck choked by his stiff collar and stud, the way his shirttails were always fouled with a brown ruck from catching between his pasty buttocks. It's not an affectionate portrait. In the bathroom, the old man's blood is still there on an old styptic pencil. He used to cut the wart on his left cheek every time he shaved. Heathcote finds a slight rise on his left cheek and begins plucking the hairs from it every day in order to aggravate it. He looks in the bathroom mirror and sees that it still carries his father's image. The fabric of the house remembers the old man, Heathcote is certain of it. This is especially true of his father's study. He sits at the desk and drums his nails on the surface, just as his father used to. It's as if he's trying to bring his father back to life. He sees ghost trails of the man's movements throughout the room, tries to absorb the old man's patterns, tries to imagine his way into the old man's head but fails. I think of myself, doing the same thing. Sitting at Heathcote's desk on the night before the funeral; chasing his ghost down the corridors at Port Eliot and into his old rooms; trying to detect his patterns, trying to imagine my way into his head, and failing—failing until, perhaps, now.

The journal follows him to France, where at the age of twenty-three he's sent to a special therapy center—ostensibly to be treated for alcoholism. Heathcote doesn't get the help he needs. It's the Wild West era of psychiatric treatment, and he has the misfortune to fall into the clutches of a therapist called Dr. Denys Kelsey and his wife, Joan Grant, a famous occultist who claimed to be the reincarnation of a previously unknown female pharaoh called Sekeeta. They hypnotize Heathcote and send him tumbling back in time through his past incarnations, searching for the moment his tortured soul was wounded. "I had been a series of odd job men," he writes. "Joan Grant was in the room to ensure that I hadn't been anyone more famous than she had been." After several sessions like this, he gets fed up and escapes to a bar in town. He's found comatose in a ditch and dragged back to the center, where he is put in a trance once more. This time the hypnotist goes in hard. Heathcote starts to seize. Someone is cutting his tongue out. When he comes around, he finds he cannot talk. You were a spy in the Spanish Civil War, they tell him. Your tongue was cut out because you refused to pass information. This left a scar on your etheric body, on your supraphysical self, which up until now you have only been able to appease with excessive drinking. "As you can imagine," Heathcote writes in the journal, "I was extremely flattered at having been allowed to have been a prisoner in the Spanish Civil War." He leaves for Paris the next day.

There he checks into a room on the sixth floor of the Hôtel d'Alsace; the same hotel, he notes in his journal, in which Oscar Wilde died. He finds it oppressive, with its panoptic design; the voices of strangers in the hallways crowd in on him. He looks out over the edge of the stairwell at the hard atrium floor far below, perhaps thinking about flying again. A peacock appears, rattling and bustling over the tiles, and then another. The concierge follows, fussily spraying their lustrous tails with some sort of liquid. Heathcote guesses it to be highly flammable hair spray. As soon as the concierge leaves the birds unattended, he begins flicking lit cigarettes down at them, trying to turn them into phoenixes.

Back home, the voice of his father explodes inside his head, calling his name. Not long after, he becomes a father for the first time himself, although you can barely tell from his papers. My sister China is born in the summer of 1969 but, as far as I can see, Heathcote hardly devotes a single sentence to the event. Elsewhere, his writings on love and sex are forceful and voluminous. But when it comes to the product of these, his pen seems to run dry. To me, his silence speaks of thoughts and feelings too unbearable to examine. It makes me think of my own silences, and the white-hot orb of terror that casts them. An orb I struggle to look at. Perhaps, in Heathcote's case, fatherhood summons the accusing ghost of his father; a child the specter of his own unhappy childhood. Things could be as simple as that—and as complicated.

China is still a baby when Heathcote abandons her and her mother to start an affair with Jean Shrimpton, the first supermodel. A *Lady and the Tramp*–type relationship. By his own admission, Heathcote goes for months at a time without seeing his child, although they all live in the same city. Jean seems to become a sort of surrogate mummy for Heathcote: she writes him checks, funds his projects, gives him a place to live. Heathcote's reaction when Jean—from his perspective—abandons him for another man is as unrestrained as a child's. There is a story, often told, about him setting himself on fire on her doorstep, whether as part of a magic trick gone wrong or as a dramatic act of self-harm it's not quite clear.

The paper trail goes dead for a few paces. When I pick it up again, it's the early 1970s and Heathcote, now thirty years old, is in Springfield Mental Hospital, in South London. There are only fragments of a picture of his time at Springfield. Scribbled clues on scraps of paper, drafts of letters, strangely boastful accounts of sexual encounters with other patients, a hint that he might have been subjected to electroconvulsive therapy. At times he seems unsure of where or when he is. He writes pleading letters to Mummy and Daddy, begging them to come pick him up, as if he's back at boarding school again. He puts these letters in envelopes addressed to Jean and her new boyfriend. A patient whom he calls Bridget the Midget lets him have sex with her in an outbuilding. He is proud of this and writes and rewrites his account of it. Sometimes he doesn't seem to take his situation very seriously. He purloins a psychiatrist's diagnostic pad and fills it out for himself.

Diagnosis: broken mojo. In other moments, he seems painfully self-aware. "I have been sent here," he scrawls across a sheet of paper, "because I killed my father."

Jean—or Mummy—visits him in the hospital but she cannot undo the harm that has been done; it's becoming clear to me that it was done long before she ever met him. After this visit, Heathcote's abjection turns to fury. He stops calling her Mummy and begins calling her other things. He pins all his anger, fear, and hatred onto her as if she is a voodoo doll of everyone who has ever hurt him. His letters become very hard to read. He threatens to scalp Jean and send her skin to someone in the Amazon whom he calls Cocaine Doris. He tells her he's blasting her with a psychic death ray visible to psychotics across the globe, who will be drawn toward her with murderous intent. He claims a Gypsy gave him the power to curse and to bless, and he curses Jean with seven years of despair and infertility. He seems to blame her, and only her, for his predicament. He is Peter Pan, he writes, and she has torn off his wings. He publishes a distillation of these letters, along with a naked photo he took of Jean, in *Suck*, the radical sex journal that Jean helped to found and fund.

After all this, China's mother, Diana, somehow finds it in herself to take Heathcote back. They have another baby in 1979, my sister Lily. Sorting through garbage bags alongside me, China finds a photo of Heathcote carrying baby Lily and squirrels it away somewhere safe. There are, she says, very few pictures of Heathcote with little Lily because, yet again, he disappears; not into the arms of another woman or an insane asylum this time, but to Port Eliot, which puts a couple hundred miles between him and his family.

There, Heathcote seems to live like a slightly dissolute monk. He never washes his clothes, or his body, or his sheets. His stink fills his wing of the house and rolls down the stairs like poison gas, curling into the nostrils of Lord Eliot. "Time for a long hot bath and to throw away some clothes," Peregrine writes in a letter he has delivered to Heathcote's rooms. "The whole house and every part therein is filled with an abomination unto the Lord." Perhaps unsurprisingly, Heathcote is able to boast about his years of celibacy.

His role at Port Eliot isn't quite that of monk, however. In letters he tells people he is a squatter, or a hermit, but the reality seems to be a little less dignified. Heathcote has to scribble for his supper. There are halfhearted poems celebrating the beauty of the seignorial chapel and the beginnings of a hagiographic history of the Eliot clan and their estates. For all his anarchistic airs, he seems to occupy an almost feudal position; somewhere between court jester and scribe.

Diana, the mother of his two daughters, writes often. Her letters are upsetting: full of tragic details of birthdays missed, of summer holidays in which the children go to visit their father and are ignored, of the grinding struggle of bringing up two little girls on her own in London and then Oxford, while Heathcote hides out on his literary oil rig. She talks about how she scrimps and saves so Heathcote doesn't have to worry about money, looks after the kids alone so he can be free from responsibilities and have the space to create. Heathcote seems to reward her by silently cutting her from his life. From her long and hurt letters, it seems like he never gives her much of an explanation, although it doesn't take her long to come up with one of her own.

It's in one of these letters that my mum makes her first appearance. Diana scrutinizes her closely at an event to promote Heathcote's new book-length poem, *Whale Nation*. Is this young and beautiful new member of Heathcote's publishing team the reason he has run out of time for her and the kids? Heathcote and my mum weren't even together at this stage, but perhaps Diana recognized a dangerous twinkle in his eye. Her letters take on an even bleaker tone: If Heathcote is having relationships with humans again, she asks plaintively that she and the children be given first right of refusal.

Heathcote keeps no journal during this period, so the only snapshots I get of him and my mum together come in these sad and, eventually, furious missives from Diana. These words make tough reading too. She doesn't seem to be able to fully blame Heathcote, so my mum gets it in the neck instead.

I appear on the scene for the first time in a letter from Heathcote's mother. She writes in the summer of 1989 to say how horrified she is at the news that Polly is pregnant. "I love you and I want to understand. I can't believe that you are prepared to ditch your family," she writes. "Please do write or talk to me. I am so dreadfully worried."

When the letters arrive in winter to congratulate Heathcote and my mum on the birth of their son, the events that follow now feel inevitable. A good magician never performs the same trick twice, but here we go for the third time. Heathcote seems condemned to repeat himself over and over again: a child a decade; a flight a decade. A mad person performing the same action and hoping for different results. Set in context, it no longer feels personal: none of it does.

This is the place I've been trying to reach. The heart of the breakdown. Leaves of paper scored deep with marks of despair are blown down the decades and into my hands. Heathcote blames my mother, blames himself, blames the ghost of his father. I see him in that room at Port Eliot, in his crow's nest at the top of the rounded tower, attacking a square of Port Eliot Estate notepaper with his calligraphic ink pen like someone trying to draw blood. He's attempting to write a letter to Ted Hughes, the poet laureate. They've corresponded before, but about each other's work; never quite like this. The words spiral around the edge of the page, crowding each other out. Heathcote's normally neat calligraphy collapses in on itself and I have to struggle to decipher individual letters as his note overspills the margins of legibility and sense.

"I'm afraid I've been ill for a year now," Heathcote scrawls. "It's family. I now have two. I have found it impossible to handle. Cracked up. I never really wanted any families! I had a strong vocation to become a Franciscan. My father put a stop to it with some brutality. I was quite young and convinced I could levitate! (There is always someone who wants to stop you flying.) I am always persuaded when things go wrong that I should have stuck to my guns. That prayer is the only media. Scrambled and fused brains. Thoughts of suicide. Pray without ceasing. Very hard."

For all the absurdity of someone confessing their suicidal thoughts to Ted Hughes, a man accused by some of having driven two of the women in his life to suicide, the letter fascinates me. Of all the items in the Archive, this is the one I will keep coming back to. Not least because an odd synchronicity seems to be at play. Ted Hughes was yet another man to share an intimate bond with the crow family, although his *Crow* was a purely literary creation. A copy of his book of crow poems winged its way to me when I was in prison, and his mythical, death-eating, God-defying bird kept me company in captivity for a while. Now, inadvertently, he brings the beginnings of some sort of release. For whatever reason, whether in search of sympathy or in an attempt to form closer ties with the man, Heathcote offers Hughes something he never managed to give me: a hint of honesty, and a sketch of an explanation. He found family impossible to handle. It made him crack up. It wasn't my fault, or my mother's fault. It wasn't even really his fault. His father's brutality made family seem like a trap, from which he sought escape. Levitation, prayer, flight, suicide. Madness can be a sort of refuge too, I suppose, although it's a refuge that won't ever truly let you go.

What can Ted Hughes have made of this letter, if Heathcote ever sent it? When I get home, I search the Internet for Ted Hughes's archives. Most of his papers seem to be locked away on the other side of the Atlantic, at Emory University. I send the librarian there an email, and she kindly replies with photocopies of Heathcote and Ted's entire correspondence. I scroll down past what I've already seen, the polite notes about each other's poems, looking for the final version of the draft confession I've been reading. It's not there. He never seems to have sent this particular letter, although there is another that dates from the period after his breakdown, after he vanished and then turned nasty on my mum.

Heathcote sent Hughes a letter containing a photo of me as a tiny baby in the bath between my mum's ankles. I'm looking up at the photographer, at Heathcote, through jet-black eyes, moonfaced; my head, half the size of my mum's foot, is pillowed on the soft flesh between her ankle and her heel. We're both naked, although the way my mum is leaning over me just about protects her modesty. Mine, less so. The flash of the camera bursts the water around us into bright shards, like a smashed mirror. Heathcote's thick handwriting edges the image, telling Ted about how all his time has been consumed by the act of caring—by being a father. It seems to me to be the version of reality he wished were true; perhaps he thought that by writing it, by believing in it, he could make it so; his truth against the world. *Y Gwir Yn Erbyn Y Byd*.

Chapter 38

I strop my bloody beak and sit back to digest. It takes a long time for this story, written in injuries, to take a shape I can make sense of. Some things I have to keep coming back to. I have to take several runs at the notes from the asylum before I can face them at all. It's unfashionable to characterize madness as a contagious disease, but that's how it feels. I get a contact high, or a contact low. My head feels hot and my thoughts crackle. Drunk as a teetotaler at a drinking party. *The power to bless and the power to curse.* I open the palm of my hand and try to summon wild birds from the air, try to conjure living flames from nothing, and am at once disappointed and relieved to discover that I am unable to. Reality will not bend to my will; the world will not shift at my word. I keep myself in check like this; remind myself that thoughts have no external power. The thing I find hardest of all about coming up against Heathcote's madness is the pure hatred that poured out of him: the hatred that he directed first toward Jean, and then later toward my mother; and, perhaps, in a less direct way, toward Diana too. I have to struggle to stop myself from simply dismissing him as an evil human being. Evil is inexplicable, and Heathcote's behavior is something I desperately need to understand.

I begin to set his story, and our story—the beginnings of this book, in fact—down in writing. Some of the similarities between us chill me: the anxiety, the paranoia, the psychotic delusions of power, the maddening itch of that one big unresolved question: Who is your daddy? And why? I think back to our strange conversations in the hospital and see him on his deathbed still chasing the ghost of his father around the chambers of his mind, carrying on an argument that should have ended decades ago. *How can you be a writer when you don't know anything?* I think about his poems, how intensely researched they were, how he had to know everything about a subject before writing about it; hardly even poems, some of them, just long lists of all the things Heathcote knew. I don't want to spend my time arguing with the dead like that, trying to prove a ghost wrong.

I turn again to the notebook the old man kept by his side at the hospital. Alongside the Welsh phrases his father drilled into him when he was a child, I discover several allusions to J. M. Barrie's *Peter Pan*: the story about the boy who could fly and who never grew up; who felt betrayed by his mother but who nevertheless kept trying to turn his girlfriend into his mother; who pushed the tyrannical father figure, Captain Hook, down to his death; who refused to return to the family home for fear he would be caught, deprived of the power of flight, and forced to become a man. A forever-child, free as a bird but trapped within his unchanging self. Perhaps, I realize, Heathcote was more self-aware than I've given him credit for. For the first time, the incredible sadness of it all comes flooding in: the tragedy of a life curtailed; an emotional life stunted; the moments when he could have been helped but was failed so badly; the shock waves that destabilized so many of the people around him, who needed him: the women in his life, his daughters, and me.

I'm nursing a coffee in the café at the end of our road, trying to unravel the knot at the heart of this story, when I suddenly get overwhelmed all over again. The act of writing somehow seems to make things real, or at least to set them in a stark new perspective. Long-submerged emotions surface unpleasantly; a great tide of past. A single thought comes to possess me. If I'm to avoid repeating the past—my own and Heathcote's—then I need help. This is more than I can manage on my own. Heathcote had help, lots of help, but it was never the right sort. It was either damaging help, like the wacky hypnosis or electroconvulsive therapy he seems to have been subjected to in the asylum, or else it was help that allowed him to remain as he was, to keep repeating the same mistakes over and over again. I need to get the sort of help he never did—help to remake myself.

Once I've had that thought, a thought years overdue, I find I cannot unthink it. For a long time now my mum has quietly and nonjudgmentally been passing on the details of therapists. I've generally paid back her kind efforts by denying that I have any problems at all, mocking the entire practice of psychotherapy, and letting their numbers and email addresses slip into the dusty corners of my phone's memory bank. Now, with something close to desperation, I search through our messages. I scroll up through the love, the concern, the jokes, the emojis, and the funny photographs—the mundane and miraculous stuff of a normal and functioning relationship—and somehow this almost moves me to tears again. I find a number, book an appointment, and feel immediate relief; relief that I no longer have to pretend to be strong, relief that I've finally admitted that I'm not necessarily okay, relief that my path and Heathcote's seem to have finally and decisively diverged. I think about him, his father, and perhaps his father before him, all unconsciously passing their damage from one generation to the next, like a family curse. I count my blessings that I'm in a position to try to begin lifting it, that I have a chance of not cursing the generation to come. I think about how many years it's taken me to get to this stage and wonder at how those with barriers to treatment far higher than any I've had to cross find the strength within themselves to do so.

As I walk back home in the cold spring sun, I notice that I feel lighter somehow. A new crack has opened up and through it has come fresh air. It's hardly a revolutionary step I've taken: a person with a history of drug psychosis, and one or two other bits of baggage besides, seeks therapy. But perhaps, sometimes, revolutionary steps—those all-consuming grand gestures—can be part of the problem. Delusions of power; the manipulation of symbols; the right word spoken at the right time causing the world to ripple. This is the opposite of that: an admission that the world has power over me. I think back to when I came out of prison; how, against all the evidence, I somehow convinced myself I had won. How, even while diving behind garbage cans, or cowering under tables, or flying into blind rages, I refused to admit I'd been in any way affected. *I stared into the abyss and the abyss blinked first.* For me, then, this is a radical step; a radical admission of humanity; of weakness; of that most hateful thing of all, vulnerability. A radical step toward normality. Prospero breaking his magic staff. Peter Pan doing the one thing he couldn't do: renouncing immortality and flight and embracing life.

When I step through the front door, I hear a suspicious clattering in the kitchen. The bird has been hard at work in my absence. She's got the broom pinned to the floor and is meticulously plucking the long, thin filaments of straw from its head. She squawks guiltily at my approach and scampers around gathering up fragments of murdered broom in her beak. I open the window and out she flies, up to the corner of the aviary where, this time last year, she began to build her first nest. I watch as she weaves the straw into place: her foundation stone. She too seems to be thinking about the next generation, in her own particular way. Repetition isn't always a bad thing, I reflect, as I think again about the coincidence of crows across generations. Heathcote's jackdaw, my magpie. Two bad-luck birds, harbingers of death, divine messengers, according to myth. But what was the message? Perhaps that, sometimes, curses can be blessings in disguise.

EGG

Chapter 39

Yana, the magpie, and I stand frozen in front of the bathroom mirror. I'm not sure how long we are stuck there, fixed dumbly in place by the sight of our own reflection. Yana is pressed close to my side, her eyes green as new moss. The bird clings to my wrist, still as taxidermy. My own eyes are black as mineshafts. The magpie breaks the spell. She opens her beak, takes a deep breath, and in a booming voice shouts "BABY!" At her word, the entire vision cracks into shards of broken glass.

It's a powerful dream. At first it seems like a simple premonition. The magpie acting as divine messenger yet again: a harbinger of life. It's around this time that Yana notices her body beginning to change. After eight months of trying to conceive a child, in mid-spring, as the birds in the trees and bushes sit on their first speckled clutches, her breasts grow and her belly gently swells around an egg, a single precious egg. I react as if someone had thrown me that egg and then forced me to run across a tight-rope with it balanced on my nose. I try to find my footing in a sort of anxious happy panic. I know this is supposed to be a joyful moment, but the cost if I were to lose my balance suddenly seems that much more severe. I'm still not convinced I'm ready for this. And then there's the terrifying vulnerability of the thing itself. The fact that neither of us actually has any real control over whether it lives or dies. As mysteriously as it arrived, it can vanish. It's almost unbearable. I compensate for this in a typically sideways manner by bringing as many tadpoles as I can catch in from the pond and feeding them vegetables and meat until our kitchen is hopping with froglets. "Yes, very nice," Yana says, when I show her, delighted. "Don't you think it's time to put them back outside now?"

Yana decides not to wait until the recommended ten-week mark, when the risk of miscarriage sharply declines, to start telling other people the news. To me this seems horribly like tempting fate, but she makes the far more practical point that if she suffers a miscarriage, she wants friends and family to know. So when people ask why she isn't drinking, she simply tells them. When people find out, they seem unreservedly happy for us. They say things like "What a lucky baby," and "You'll be a great dad." At first I find their confidence perplexing, and then, slowly, as I realize they aren't lying, that their belief is genuine, it begins to seem almost reassuring.

The real-life magpie, not wanting to be outdone, puts the finishing touches on her nest and promptly lays half a dozen eggs. She proudly announces each one as it appears, trumpeting their arrival from the parapet of her twig castle as if they're speckle-headed dignitaries entering the court of a mighty queen. She seems to want me to share in her glory, so one morning, very slowly, I reach my hand up into the mossy bowl at the heart of her nest. I feel the eggs beneath my fingertips. Warm and unsettlingly greasy. The magpie perches on my shoulder and chatters away unconcernedly, so, very carefully, I lift one of the eggs from the nest and bring it down to eye level. It is a perfect thing, a pale verdigris orb only a little larger than my middle knuckle. I press it gently against the tip of my nose and then return it to the nest.

Yana and the magpie are both changed creatures. Benzene refuses to leave her nest and Yana—never normally one for lounging around—begins to spend an uncharacteristically long time in bed, as if weighed down by the grain of life inside her. I try to be the best husband I can to both. In the mornings, as I make tea to bring up to Yana, the bird yammers at me through the window, demanding to be fed where she sits. The painful truth is that I'm not quite bird enough for one, and still not quite human enough for the other. Yana quietly begins training one of her sisters to be there at the birth, just in case.

Birds and babies become ever more entwined in my head. Most nights I dream of little black birds. Not soaring away through the sky with me on their back, as I often have in the past; these dream-birds are flightless chicks that sit helplessly in the palm of my hand. I protect them and nurture them. Sometimes they're still only eggs; then I have to keep them warm in my armpits or balance them in nests woven tenuously into my hair.

Benzene's eggs will never hatch, no matter how long she warms them. I take one away and shine a flashlight through it just to make sure she hasn't somehow mated through a gap in her enclosure. Through the speckled green of the shell I see the shadow of the yolk and, much to my relief, nothing more. I return the egg to the nest and watch as the magpie gently nudges it into place alongside the others and then lowers herself onto the clutch like an old man settling into a comfy armchair. One day we'll try to find a mate for her; another similarly eccentric magpie must somewhere exist. But, for now, an imminent human baby is enough to contend with.

In May the anniversary of the day the bird arrived in our lives comes around again. Her second year with us. Two years longer than she would have lived had Yana's sister not scooped her out of the gutter and brought her home. In that time she's been many things: companion, muse, grief counselor, bluebottle hunter, and mouse catcher. She's seen sorrow, and she's seen joy. She's had a bird's-eye view of my life, but I still have no idea what she really thinks of me. Mobile perch. Food dispenser. Vanquisher of bothersome cats. From the determination with which she clings to my head, I'd like to think she's fond of me; but then, equally, she could just be waiting hungrily for me to drop dead. Her mind is so other, I can only guess what she's thinking as my mum, my dad, my grandmother, siblings, and friends pour through the door for a celebratory lunch of homemade Chinese food and worms. If we seem strange to her—her mountainous, featherless family—she doesn't let on. Benzene is, in fact, as perfect a host as a magpie can be. She leaves her nest for the first time in weeks and marches across the table, stabbing dumplings and getting grains of rice stuck to her beak.

"Do you think she knows?" my grandmother says. "Dogs and cats always seem to."

"I haven't noticed her being any more affectionate than usual," Yana says drily, as Benzene crushes one of her birthday grubs to death with a quick snap of her beak.

"And how will the bird and the baby get along?" my grandmother asks.

Benzene seems to have been waiting for this question for a while. Her timing is too perfect. Before Yana or I can answer she leaps onto my dad's head, opens her beak, and lets out a flawlessly human laugh. We are all awestruck. The bird laughs twice more and then zips her beak. No matter how hard we try to provoke her, she refuses to laugh again.

Her maniac's chuckle isn't a wholly reassuring answer to my grandmother's question, a question I've been fretting over too. Benzene can be careless with her beak, and babies are so very soft. Perhaps the dream about the magpie in the mirror contained another prophecy too: The arrival of the baby will finally shatter our interspecies family setup. My dad suggests getting the baby a tiny beekeeper's outfit; my mum mimes the wringing of a tiny magpie neck.

"It'll be fine," Yana says, waving their worries away. "When the baby's asleep, the bird can come in; when the baby's awake, the bird will go back outside. We'll just have to be good at juggling."

Magpies, crows, and jackdaws begin to fall from the trees; youngsters tumbling from their nests as they do every spring. People contact me—friends and strangers—to say they've found these juvenile birds, asking me to help. If they seem uninjured and the parents are still around, I tell them to put them back in their trees. If not, I do what probably should have been done with Benzene and call in the experts: wildlife rescuers who devote their lives to helping animals in the right way, even ones as hated as crows, magpies, and jackdaws.

The carrion crows in the garden don't escape my bird-baby complex. They've built their nest up in the neighbor's sycamore again, an unruly pile of sticks balanced in a bough just beyond the farthest tendril of the ivy that climbs the trunk of the tree. Last year, their nest failed, but this year there seem to be eggs. The female spreads herself protectively over them like a thick black blanket while the male forages for food. The eggs hatch and the chicks make themselves known to me with their hungry cries. I watch over them obsessively, as if by keeping them safe I can make my own luck. I leave out plates of scrambled eggs and glistening piles of raw chicken liver and then watch as the mother fills her crop and returns to her nest. She dips her oiled beak tenderly into the shadows. Before too long, three dusty black heads appear over the edge of the nest. Blue-eyed baby crows, just about clinging to life.

A few weeks after this, our baby first becomes visible. At the local hospital, an ultrasound technician lights up Yana's insides. Yana lies down on a bed and rolls up her top to allow one of the operators to smear conductive goo on her belly. On the screen in front of us, indistinct shapes slide over each other and then resolve into that of a tiny, misshapen human. The creature squirms and kicks like a prawn. Yana laughs with delight. "Baby is very active in there," the technician says cheerily, and then proceeds to take us on a white-knuckle ride through the body of our unborn child. She counts off organs and limbs as we go. Heart—yep. Kidneys one and two. Stomach all there. One hand. Two hands. I look on agog, aghast, waiting for something to be missing. Yana just carries on smiling and laughing.

"Your baby has a beautiful spine," the technician says, oddly.

The baby is seven centimeters from head to toe, the size of a sardine. I hold out my hand to visualize it and see that it could curl easily into my cupped palm. On the screen, a face appears, a profile that fades in and out, from surface to skull to brain. The technician measures it: the baby's head is just two centimeters across, as small and delicate as a songbird's egg.

When we get home, I pass out on the sofa. Anyone would think that I was the pregnant one. In my sleep I pick an egg from Benzene's nest and hold it in the palm of my hand. At my touch, its beautiful shine fades away. The egg rots, and then cracks, and its contents spill out like guts from a slit belly. I wake full of fear.

Since starting therapy, dreams like this have been coming thick and fast, almost tailor-made for the shrink's couch, although I don't think I need professional help to guess what this one means. I take myself out into the garden. The two adult crows gronk their greetings. All three of their babies survived and fledged the nest and are now spread out across the branches of the sycamore trees like fat black candles. They still have their incredible blue eyes, and they still beg noisily for food. I put out a plate of old sausages for them and then sit very still and watch.

The crows see what I've done and begin to stir in their branches. Even though this is a well-practiced routine, they still approach by cautious increments. Today, they're just too slow. A wild magpie shoots recklessly in from behind an elderflower bush and begins to hammer at the sausages. I've seen this bird before; I recognize it by its unusually pronounced beak and its strange manner. It likes to hang upside down on the neighbor's bird feeder, sometimes it comes and stares at me through the window, and sometimes, I'm quite sure, it comes into the kitchen and throws things onto the floor. The crows respond with shouts of anger and the mother shoots like a cannonball at the beaky magpie. To my astonishment, the wild magpie races toward me. I look slowly down and find it seeking safety between my feet.

Chapter 40

It is August on the farm, unmistakably so: the lavender beds are softly humming to themselves, the lawn is dying for a drink, and the spindly old greengage tree has crowned itself with emeralds again. But which August is it, exactly? I feel like I've stood in this exact spot, at this exact moment, every summer for a hundred years. The landscape seems like a rolling backdrop: always changing, always repeating; an eternal loop. I have to remind myself that it's an illusion. There are no true repeats in nature. I pick out the threads of the particular. The fist-sized holes in the trunk of the greengage tree, calling card of the local woodpeckers; the high-pitched keening of a red kite coming from somewhere beyond the horse paddock—the first, my dad claims, he's spotted here in twenty years; the shifting society of crows, rooks, magpies, and jackdaws, individuals all, living their complex lives alongside ours.

The ecology within me has shifted too. Heathcote's death has, in a strange way, washed the landscape clean. Picking over his entrails made me feel sick at first, but then I arranged them in a pattern that made sense and I began to feel a whole lot better. Madness doesn't run in the blood and it doesn't just strike like lightning. It too has its threads, its deep roots in the particular. Clearly, I've had my own moments of mental volatility, and perhaps I always will. A crack, once made, is hard to fully close. But it's not because of the blood that runs in my veins. We all have our own deep roots grounded in the past, darkly guiding our present. You can't sever yourself from your past but perhaps, if you dig around a little, you can excavate some of its power. Expose those roots to the heat of the sun. Let them wither.

This very simple and obvious realization has made me feel lighter again, as if a weight I didn't even know existed has lifted from the top of my head. Heathcote's ghost is finally beginning to evaporate—the phantom I've been trying to grasp hold of for so many years is beginning to let loose its hold on me. When I first wanted to get to know him, back when I was a kid, it was partly because I wanted to get to know myself. I thought that in him I could see my own future, my own nature. Now that I've gotten to know him, it has helped me to know myself, but not in the way I imagined. Who your father is isn't who you have to be. Nurture trumps nature. It has to.

I look back toward the house. The magpie is watching me through one of the ground-floor windows, a sentient shadow. Her nest and eggs are long forgotten. It happened in an instant. One day she was a protective mother guarding her clutch, the next I woke to find her jumping on my head demanding to play, and the next day her molt began. Worn black feathers fall and are replaced. She sheds her past, long past its use, and grows anew. Tomorrow, she flies free. Except for a few accidental excursions out through the front door and onto the street, she hasn't flown truly free since the Christmas before last, when the experts on the Crow Forum warned us that, for a bird as tame as her, freedom could spell death. I've been a willing accomplice in her confinement, only too ready to agree that the world is a dangerous place. Over a year indoors. It doesn't seem fair. She's been a prisoner of my anxieties long enough. It's time to let go and have faith that she'll come back, if that's what she wants. There won't be any harnesses, or tethers, or falconry techniques. Happiness, freedom, these things involve risk. Sometimes safety can be a padded cell. I've taken what measures I can. It might not be entirely scientific, but I've been using the wild crows and magpies as a sort of barometer: recently they stopped attacking each other on sight, a sign that the warlike mentality that accompanies breeding season has begun to soften, which I'm hoping means it's a good time to fly an unattached bird. It's to be an exercise in trust—although whether it's more for her benefit or my own I'm not entirely certain.

Yana emerges and joins me where I stand by the garden gate. She too has undergone changes. She's slowly growing as round as the pears that are just starting to ripen on the trees in the orchard. Small things make her lachrymose: the sound of a baby crying; a video of an orphaned monkey that someone posts on Facebook; people who offer up their seats on the bus. We take the dirt track down to the river. It allegedly follows the route of an old Roman road, and every time I walk it I keep my eyes to the ground at least part of the way, hoping for a hairpin, a ring, a coin, a horseshoe. One year we even probed it with a metal detector but the only trinkets it seems to hold are old bottle caps and discarded sections of pipe and wire. Magpie treasures.

Around the bend we encounter a family of roe deer; a doe in her red summer coat and two fawns half her size who do their best to hide behind her as they dash to the safety of an island of young oaks and brambles. All three watch us from the shadows. From somewhere to our right, a buzzard mewls. When I look back to the deer, they're halfway to a distant hedgerow, their three white tails bobbing through the air like doves in flight.

In front of us, the water meadow has been dashed black by a crowd of rooks, crows, and jackdaws. All these birds have their own collective nouns: a murder of crows, a parliament of rooks, a clattering of jackdaws. But how to describe corvid conferences such as these? Seeing our approach, they all take off as one, as suddenly as if we'd run at them screaming and shouting and clapping our hands instead of strolling sedately in their direction as we are. A sprinkling of feathers remains where they were gathered, as if they'd been in such a hurry to leave that they forgot to get properly dressed. Late summer is to corvids what autumn is to trees. I pick the feathers up as I come across them and press them to my nose. Crow feathers stink, or at least these long, sturdy wing feathers do, like unwashed hair and mutton grease. The smaller flight feathers I find, jackdaw feathers, have a quite different aroma: hot from the sun, they give off a sweet, somewhat heady scent that is strangely familiar. Jackdaw feathers smell just like church incense, as if they all roost above altars. At the center of their parade ground, a small, sad object lies coiled up in the grass: the head and torso of a fawn. Its limbs—the profitable parts—have been hacked off and carried away by the poachers who shot it. Scavengers are making quick work of the rest. Its eyes are gone, its rib cage unzipped, its lips pecked away to a snarl. I remember another collective noun I've heard people use for carrion birds that seems appropriate for the coroners' feast that we appear to have interrupted: a wake of corvids. It's an ambiguous augury.

The grass on the riverbank's gentle slope seems confused by its own proximity to water, scorched brown in places, lush green in others, as if sewn from a huge strip of army camouflage material. Yana lies down in the shade of a willow and soon falls asleep. She sleeps a lot these days and I wonder if her naps correspond to the baby's—whether the other person living inside her is sleeping now too, or whether the unborn is simply sucking the energy out of her, draining the grid like an electricity thief and diverting it toward some sort of secret project, like the construction of a brain.

I slip out of my clothes and approach the water. Nettles tower along the edge, woven together by creeping bindweed, a plant prettier than its name. It flowers here and there, soft white trumpets that hypnotize bees with their sweet, silent tune. Damselflies flit between garish spears of purple loosestrife, snapping their mandibles at the mosquitoes and gnats that hover over the slowly flowing river.

I take five quick breaths to prepare myself for the cold and slide into the water, my flesh leaping like a scalded frog as I breaststroke inelegantly to the far bank and come to rest by a patch of water lilies. With the tips of my toes, I can just about touch the bottom. I root myself there and look about with eyes just above the water's surface, froglike. Lily pads as big as dinner plates play host to resting damselflies, their capillaried wings tucked neatly behind their backs, and fat, lazy hoverflies. The sun is pouring into the river at a slant, lighting up the lilies' long, slimy stems, which vanish nevertheless into darkness, as spooky as anchor chains or deep-sea pipelines.

I push off back out into the middle of the river and tread water. Here the riverbed is far out of reach. I expel the air from my lungs and allow myself to sink. This dirty river has washed so many moments clean. I descend slowly, but the light fades fast, from golden brown to murky green to inkwell black as my feet hit the bottom and my body falls slowly backward. I feel the soft riverbed with my palms, the backs of my arms, my legs; it cushions my spine, a silky membrane of sediment. The sun is hidden away behind the thick blanket of water that covers me, barely prickling through. I am cocooned. In my ears, the double rhythm of my heartbeat thuds faintly and the current seems to murmur as it passes. From somewhere, I hear—or I imagine I hear—the voice of a woman. The words, if they are words, are garbled and indistinct. This, I think vaguely, must be what it's like to be in the womb. And then: no more thoughts. Silence floods in; the internal silence I crave, as addictive as any drug. I don't know how long I remain like that: perhaps seconds, perhaps minutes. My mind is totally adrift. I feel like I could happily stay down here for hours. And then, suddenly, something shifts. The darkness that was so comforting is now terrifying. The bottom of the river is the last place on earth I want to be. I squirm upright and kick my way back toward the light, sucking air into my lungs as greedily as someone resurrected.

Up on the bank, Yana is still asleep, softly snoring while in the background the eternal soundtrack plays: a wood pigeon trills and coos, a buzzard blows the same two notes over and over again, rough as a recorder or a pennywhistle, and the crows and rooks rasp away at the bass notes. Yana's rounded belly is bare to the sun, terrifyingly exposed, like an egg without a shell. Her skin ripples as, beneath the surface, something stirs and kicks with life.

That evening, we make a fire up by the house and wait for the barn owl to start its waking rounds. My dad is busy greasing a frying pan and stoking the fire; my grandmother sits in the middle of a wooden bench blasting Icelandic rock music through a pair of leaky white headphones; and my mum is over by the garden gate smoking. Behind her, hidden in the thick wisteria that hugs the house, a wood pigeon rustles around.

"They build their nest there every year," my mum says, "and every year that fat cat reaches out the window and swipes their chicks."

Yana sits by the fire with a bundle of sticks in her lap, lengths of ash that we collected from the woods earlier in the day. Using a small, sharp knife, she shears off the bark, exposing the clean white wood underneath, ribs for the crib we are building. I join in and my dad, unable to resist an opportunity to show off his tools, fetches an old cast-iron plane from his shed and does so too. Here and there, small holes appear in the wood—it's already nursed numerous beetle larvae through their early stages of life—and soon the grass beneath our feet is covered with long, thin strips of bark. Yana gathers the shorn sticks and demonstrates how they will slot together, neater and cleaner than the pigeon's nest, certainly, but not—to my mind—so very different in principle.

Conversation somehow turns from the cradle to the grave. My parents seem to see their own end in this new beginning. My mum starts issuing instructions for her funeral, pointing out where exactly on the farm she'd like us to bury her body—ideally right next to the dogs—and which poems each of her children is to read. My dad claims he wants to be thrown on the compost heap and left there for the worms, and my grandmother pops off her headphones to ask if there's room for her on the compost too. Like the ticking clock inside the crocodile, this baby-to-be seems to have set the older generation's thoughts to death, as if the planet has a one-in-one-out door policy. The old must be shed—or thrown on the compost—so the new can grow. They seem happy about it, though: happier, perhaps, than I've ever seen them.

The wood pigeon rustles around again in the wisteria and then flies from its nest. Even with my eyes closed I could tell what sort of bird it is. Its stiff flight feathers sing through the air. It whistles and hums over our heads, its chest a smear of pastel pink, heading out to forage seeds and grain for its two chicks. They haven't been eaten by the cat this year—at least not yet.

The next morning I seek out Benzene. I find her in the living room, gazing out across the valley from atop a pile of books. Outside the sky is overcast; spittle flecks the window. Perhaps conditions aren't quite right, I think hopefully. The bird flies from my hand to the windowsill and back, squeaks. Impassable chasm of language and species aside, it's obvious what she's saying.

I walk through the house with the bird on my wrist. She bobs up and down, trying to see all things from all angles, her talons pressing into my flesh. Every time we round a corner, I feel her grip tighten as she braces for the unknown, and then as shapes and shadows resolve into harmless objects she slowly lets go. In the kitchen her eyes absorb the familiar faces of Yana, my mum, and my dad. They follow behind as I pass through the library toward the double doors at the back of the house. The bird sharpens to a point, like a spear threatening the sky. I think of everything she has given me, say a prayer that she will remember the same, and then throw open the doors. She may return. She may not. Her choice. I'm letting go.

The bird shoots out and up. The touch of an unfamiliar easterly breeze causes her to wobble in the sky but she soon corrects herself. She's a natural. I've learned more from this bird than I can possibly say. She's taught me new ways of seeing, new ways of caring; and the limits of care too. There are mistakes I've made with her that I'll have to make sure not to repeat in the future. Care can be taken too far and become captivity. Now, as she soars above our heads, she conducts a master class in the joy of simply being. That's what flying is, or at least what it is to me. Flying is to exist in nothing but the moment; to be present without a thought of the past, the future a wing beat away. I sprint after her, underneath her, flying along with the bird as she passes over the top of the greengage tree, loops around the crabapple, over the ditch, and into the field beyond. I crash through the flower beds, leap the fence, and wade out into the waist-deep greenery, grinning in her wake. The magpie rejoices in the air. It is her element.

Chapter 41

Two days after Christmas, Yana wakes from a dream. A soul is knocking on the door, demanding to be let in; behind it, the ghost of a Victorian baby carriage fades away. It's just before dawn and, from the wetness spreading out beneath her, she guesses that her water has broken. She lies still for a while and feels the electric pulses of her first contractions pass through her body. A soul is knocking.

As the sun rises, and the magpie begins to sing her morning song, Yana nudges me awake. I make tea, fetch towels, and begin to slowly fill the birthing pool as Yana breathes heavily through each contraction. We think we're prepared for this: We've been to the classes, learned the self-hypnosis techniques, and practiced the calming mantras. Yana has spent countless evenings visualizing herself as a rosebud softly opening; as a ripple spreading out on a calm pond; as a hot-air balloon floating effortlessly away. I hold her hand and try some of those techniques now. Yana farts, then another contraction hits and she makes a noise with her mouth that sounds like a horse whiffling. With the sweat, and the heat, and the strange sweet smells—and, of course, the noises—our room begins to feel like a stable. With each contraction, Yana seems to retreat from me and perhaps even from herself; she becomes the animal thing that is happening to her, that she is doing.

When the contractions reach a certain frequency, I text the number we were given by the local National Health Service home birthing unit. An hour later two midwives arrive: one tall, thin, and gray-haired; the other short, fat, and smelling of cigarettes. The senior midwife, Sadie, gets out a stylish leather-handled stopwatch and times Yana's contractions, then performs a quick examination.

"Beautiful," Sadie says. "Beautiful. You are brilliant at this. The baby is a finger-length away. It will be here very soon."

Yana gets into the birthing pool, gets out again, walks up and down the stairs, lowers herself into the bath and hauls herself out again, squats, lunges, desperately tries to pee, groans, swears, grunts. Still no baby. The sun passes over the top of the house and streams through the bedroom windows, lighting up wisps of steam that rise from the surface of the birthing pool. One of the baby's limbs presses out from behind Yana's belly button and shows no sign of moving any farther down. Yana's entire body shakes with the force of the contractions. The sun disappears over the rooftops and the baby's heart rate takes a dip.

"That's a very tired baby," says Sadie. "I think it's time to go to the hospital."

Blue lights illuminate the street. I walk Yana out to the ambulance and help her get strapped into the stretcher, taking a seat alongside her, together with Sadie and a jolly paramedic. As we speed along the backstreets to the nearby hospital, I feel myself beginning to panic. I start thinking about what my life will be like without Yana, how every single beautiful thing she has made will fall to bits in my hands and the baby will have nothing to remember its mother by. Tears start to brim in my eyes. I try to wind it back in, for Yana's sake, although I clearly don't quite succeed because Sadie takes a moment to squeeze my arm.

"Everything is going to be fine," she says. "You don't need to worry."

When we get to the hospital, Yana waves the waiting wheelchair away and insists on half staggering to the elevator, using me to prop herself up, until the orderly gets so frustrated with the pace that he scoops her into the chair and wheels her rapidly to an assessment room. Yana lies panting on a hospital bed as nurses buzz around her, checking her vitals and hooking her up to a bank of blinking machines. An exhausted-looking doctor performs an ultrasound. The baby has turned the wrong way around, she tells us. She recommends going into the operating room immediately: forceps first, and cesarean if that doesn't work. She doesn't give the impression that she wants to stand around for long weighing the various pros and cons.

"What do you want to do?" she asks Yana.

Yana closes her eyes and her whole body seizes up as another contraction hits her.

"I don't know," she gasps.

I ask the doctor to come away to the side. All of this is so far removed from the home birth we had planned for.

"Is there any way . . . What would happen if we let things progress as they are?" I ask. "Do you think it would be possible to give her a little time and see what happens?"

"This is my bread and butter," the doctor says, somewhat sharply. "She needs to go into the operating room."

She turns back to Yana.

"It will take half an hour to get the operating room ready, so I need an answer now."

Yana gives her assent and the doctor departs rapidly from the room. Things move very quickly after that. The nurses remove Yana's necklaces and tape over her wedding rings; the anesthetist comes to explain exactly what a spinal is; another nurse asks her to sign consent forms for the various procedures they might have to carry out: forceps delivery; episiotomy; cesarean section. I am given a set of well-worn blue scrubs to pull over my clothes and then we make our way to the operating room. Sadie stays with us all the way.

In the operating room, the doctor is waiting. In the last half hour, she has transformed from a worryingly exhausted individual to a person alive with electrical energy. Her eyes shine with something close to zeal as Yana is wheeled center stage beneath the bright overhead lights.

I sit in a plastic chair by Yana's head and hold her hand, careful not to disturb the catheter that feeds some sort of clear solution into her arm. Yana's hand grips mine tight as another contraction hits, this one seemingly stronger than any that have come before. She grips with such force that blood shoots out of her arm into the catheter, up the plastic tube, and into the bag of clear liquid, turning it pink. One of the nurses whistles and admires her strength. Between contractions the anesthetist attempts to administer a spinal injection with a long, thin needle. He struggles with it for a while. Yana's back muscles are, he says, like a rock. Eventually he finds a fissure and slides the needle home.

"And that," he says, with satisfaction, "is the last contraction you will feel."

As Yana's legs are strapped into a pair of stirrups, a nurse squirts different parts of her body with a cold spray and asks if she can feel anything, explaining that cold and pain work on the same receptors.

I try to keep my features composed but am horrified by all of this. The needle in the spine. The bright surgical instruments. The entire environment so reminiscent of tragedy and death. Luckily Yana's eyes are closed, because I can feel how empty my face is of blood. Sadie comes over and touches me on the shoulder.

"Look at all the smiling, chatting people in the room," she says—a little impatiently this time. "Do you think we'd all be smiling if this wasn't going to be perfectly straightforward?"

I snap out of it, smile, and give Yana's hand a gentle squeeze. She squeezes mine back as the doctor and her assistant make their way toward her with some sort of surgical jack, which they stick inside her to prop her open—and then in go the forceps.

Yana, thankfully, can't see, but I can. I wasn't prepared for how brutal a forceps delivery would be. The doctor is not gently wobbling and tugging, like someone easing out a loose tooth. When Yana's contractions come, the doctor leans back—seemingly with all her weight—more like a sailor hauling in the rigging than a surgeon trying to guide a baby toward the light. And it's not just one or two pulls. It's one after the other. Each time the machine beeps to indicate a coming contraction, the doctor gets a new cross-hands grip, making an X with her wrists, and leans deep into it, so far and so hard that I'm worried she's going to pull the baby's head off, or crush it like a fresh nut.

"The next one," says Sadie. "The baby will be here on the next one."

Another push, a pull, a spurt of blood, and out from between Yana's legs comes something purple, swollen, seemingly lifeless; a barely human-looking head, and a tiny torso. They rush it immediately away and put out an urgent call for the baby doctor. *Why*, I dimly wonder, *wasn't the baby doctor already in the room?* I hadn't noticed it until now, but in the corner of the operating room is a replica of the array around Yana, but scaled down: a tiny hospital bed, with wires and tubes leading to a small bank of monitoring equipment. The baby, still purple and motionless, lies there surrounded by medical staff in their blue gowns and thin green hats, cleaning and rubbing it. One of them fits a tiny, espresso cup–sized oxygen mask over its mouth.

"They're just trying to get her breathing," someone says. "The cord was wrapped around her neck." *Daughter*, I think. *Not breathing*. Yana and I wait under the lights in the center of the room; for how long I don't know. Time loses all meaning. Then a weak, gravelly, quavering voice pierces the air. My eyes fill with tears at the noise, as do Yana's. Tears of joy and relief.

"Come on," says one of the nurses. "Come and say hello to your daughter."

I go and look at her properly for the first time. She's moving vigorously, waving her arms and kicking at the center of a swirl of doctors and prodding fingers. Her face is bruised from where the forceps latched over her eyes and onto her cheeks, but even so she already looks very familiar, a total stranger whom I instantly recognize. Dark hair, button nose, pointy chin. Only one of her eyes is open, the other is swollen shut. I look at it—the deep mineral blue of a flooded slate mine—and begin to talk to her. She tracks the sound of my voice, homing in on me. I hold out my forefinger and she clasps it in her hand. A nurse hands me a pair of surgical scissors and I cut off the excess foot or so of umbilical cord, then I lift her over to the scales to be weighed, and then finally to Yana's chest: a long, stressful journey to a destination so close to her point of origin. Yana kisses her for the very first time and puts her finger in the baby's hand to be gripped too.

"She should have a strong, powerful name," one of the nurses says. "Because that took a lot of strength."

An orderly wheels Yana and the baby up to the neonatal ward.

There, in the far corner by the window, I watch the baby take her first drink of milk from Yana's breast. Yana gasps with the intensity of it. We pass the baby back and forth, marveling at her. When she cries, she does so very quietly and her bottom lip quivers in a way that somehow makes me love her even more than I realize I already do. Yana sleeps with the sleeping baby curled up on her chest. I watch them both from the chair by the bed, seeing the way the baby occasionally startles as some dream or noise or nervous calibration strikes her, and then I pass out too.

I wake in the early hours to the sound of the baby crying. I check her diaper and find that it's full of thick black goo. I change her, then sit back down in the chair and cradle her while Yana sleeps on. Her head fits neatly into my palm.

The night around us is full of strange noises. Other babies screaming and grunting. The *tic-tac-tic-tac* of bed curtains being drawn like mice scrabbling along the ceiling. The clatter and crash of scaffolding being erected outside. The heavy rumble of passing buses. In the dim yellow light, I stare down at the baby nestled quietly in my arms and everything else fades away. Through her single mysterious blue eye she stares back up at me. Our faces are inches from each other. I can hear her irregular, panting breathing as she gets a handle on her lungs and diaphragm, and she can feel my hot breath on her face, feel the reassuring rhythm of my heart as it thumps away beneath her. All I can think is how much I love this person, how much I want to protect her, how I will always be there for her as best I can. An invisible bond is formed, one that can never be broken.

Epilogue

One day in early spring the magpie disappears. She does it right in front of me, although I feel it more than I see it: a cold wind on the back of my neck, a wingtip against my cheek as she rushes past me toward the narrowing gap in the door. One moment she's there, perched in a sunny spot in her aviary on the farm, her feathers burning blue and gold like an alchemist's fire, the next she's gone, leaving only empty space behind. I spin around in time to see her soaring up over the chicken enclosure and into the sky. I should be used to her flights of fancy by now. The bird flies away, the bird returns. But this is very clearly different from any of her past flights. Benzene is determined. I hold out my arm and whistle and wait for the invisible tether to start tugging. Benzene carries on flying. It takes me another second to realize that she has no intention of coming down. She's higher than the oaks, higher than the airy tip of a cloudlike poplar. I watch, horrified, as other magpies emerge from bushes and trees to scold and squabble with her as they defend their territory. She spins in a double helix with another bird, both of them snapping and yammering at each other until they reach a peak and disentwine.

I stumble into ditches and dive through tiny gaps in hedgerows, trying to keep my eyes fixed on her diminishing dot. I burst through a bush and surprise a buzzard. Rabbits scatter. Wild magpies fly unhelpfully to and fro, each one making me less certain that I'm chasing the right bird. Different dots pull in different directions and soon I no longer know which one to follow. She kaleidoscopes into a dozen birds.

On the top of a ridge overlooking the farm I realize that I've lost her; this time perhaps for good. As I make my way back toward the aviary, panting and sweating, I ask everyone I meet if they've seen a magpie. The farm is being given a spring spruce-up and is a hive of activity. The carpenters fixing up a rotten gate are kind enough to take my question seriously, although I barely stop myself from shrieking at the absurdity of it. Of course they've seen a magpie. Everyone's seen a magpie. I pick twigs from my hair and lick the thorn scratches on my forearms clean.

Back near the chickens, I hear a familiar chirrup. I smile. That old trick again. Benzene is low in the branches of an oak tree, picking at moss. I whistle. She jumps higher into the tree, leaping as nimbly as a monkey up to the canopy and out of sight again. I jog over a carpet of bluebells and out into the middle of a grassy field to get a better view. The magpie sits at the highest point of the oak, dripping gold in the sun. The oak's newly unfurled leaves seem almost liquid in this light; fresh and wet as an emergent luna moth's wings. Benzene clucks cheerfully as they flutter around her. I stand with both arms outstretched and try to summon her down to me like some sort of mixed-up scarecrow. She chirrups and spins around to face the horizon.

"What should I do?" I ask Yana when she calls from the house to find out where I've got to.

"Well," she says. "What can you do?"

I have to admit she has a point. I suppose what I'm really trying to ask is how should I feel. We've been told over and over that a tame magpie is unlikely to survive in the wild, although I've seen this one kill enough insects, mice, and even the odd unlucky frog to know she is more than capable of finding her own food. She appears to be snacking on something right now: a woodlouse or a beetle that she's dug out of a furrow in the bark. She snaps her beak and sways with her branch in the breeze. Up there in her tree, she seems calmer and more content than she's been for months, since the baby came along and knocked her a peg down the pecking order. She seems happy.

"Maybe that's your answer then," Yana says. "You should feel happy."

The magpie leads me from tree to tree down into the valley, through more bushes and hedgerows and finally into a bog. There, with my feet half sunk in the ground, she swoops down at last and lands on my arm. I think about catching her in my hand and taking her home, but I can't bring myself to do it. I try to capture every detail of her instead. The gentle touch of her talons. The unexpected warmth of her feet. Her eyes: once grotto blue, now river brown in the sun. The impossible petrochemical shimmer of her feathers: the shifting bands of green, gold, purple, and blue making her a different bird from every angle. She strops her beak against my wrist one final time, then with a shrug of her wings she takes off. There's no following her this time. I track her through the sky like a dark star as she arcs over the lake, over the river, toward the smoky purple of the woods. She cuts through the air toward the distant horizon and then, like a comet winking out of existence, she's gone.

Under the apple tree in front of the house Yana sits on a blanket with the baby lying next to her. She's hung a mobile from a low branch and tiny sailboats spin in the breeze above the baby's head. The bruises from her forceful birth have long since faded and both eyes are wide open. Their color seems to change depending on which angle you see them from. Sometimes they're mineral blue, sometimes green, sometimes nut brown, as if they're still deciding. At my approach, the baby's eyes slide from the sailboats to me: right now, at this particular moment, they appear deep blue with flecks of gold. Registering my familiar face, the baby's mouth breaks into a gummy grin. She sticks out her tongue like a yawning cat and I nuzzle her under her pointy nubbin of a chin. The faces of her ancestors seem to flash across hers like a wheel of fortune: Sometimes I'm surprised to see the face of my beloved late grandfather looking up at me from the baby blanket, sometimes it's my grandmother, sometimes pudgy versions of Yana or me. There's no denying that Heathcote is in there too. In her more solemn moments, she seems like that little boy in the picture nervously clutching his apple, although I no longer see that as the curse I once might have. Four months old, the baby contains ghost-prints of all of these people but, above all, she is exactly herself.

A pair of wings whistles overhead. Wood pigeon. Despite Yana giving me permission to be happy about Benzene's departure, I already know I'm going to spend the next few days fruitlessly chasing magpies around the farm. And so I see Benzene everywhere: every blackbird, jackdaw, rook, wood pigeon, every low-flying magpie is, for an instant, her. I hear her in the outraged honks of the ducks having their shiniest feathers plucked, in the distant yap of a dog having its tail tugged or, perhaps, its anus pecked, in the helium-pitched scolding of the blue tits. Perhaps that's the point, Yana says. Benzene is just another bird now, and no bird will be just a bird ever again.

Eventually, after a week searching the sky, we have to go back home. When we arrive I throw open the doors to the aviary and sweep the bird's treasures into a corner. Magpie days are over, I think. Featherhood finishes as fatherhood begins—or so I mistakenly believe.

Before dawn the next day, while Yana and the baby are both still asleep, I creep silently out of bed and down the stairs, past the carriage in the hallway to the kitchen, where I sit and write. Heathcote was at least partly correct about one thing: Writing demands a vanishing act. I have to find moments to disappear, ways to cut myself off. But never completely. I always come back. Yana and the baby stop me from flying away, and that is a very good thing indeed. I look up from my keyboard to see the sun spilling through the trees. The aviary, which yesterday seemed so empty, is dappled with golden-green light and brimming with songbirds. Robins, wrens, tits, and sparrows have poured in through the open door and are singing on the branches where another bird once perched.

Meanwhile, at a scrapyard a few miles west of the farm, a magpie flutters to the ground. Around it broken cars are stacked in rough lines, engines and exhaust pipes lie in piles, and puddles of petrochemicals shine purple in the morning light. The bird seems strangely at home in this all too human environment. At first the two mechanics don't notice the creature standing so fearlessly at their feet. They carry on stripping the valuable parts from an old Mini Cooper, singing along to the radio as they work. The bird quacks tunelessly along with them as it struts along the forecourt tossing around wrenches and bolts. The mechanics stop what they're doing and stare. It's a magpie, but a magpie unlike any they've ever seen before. One of them gets out his phone and starts filming. The bird stops its strutting and stares right back at them. It opens its beak.

"Come on!" it says. "Come on!"

Useful Information

Before attempting to rescue an animal, it's important to make sure that it is truly in need of assistance. Many birds leave their nests days before they can fly. They may look helpless or abandoned but they are often still being taken care of by their parents. Unless the animal is sick, or injured, or in obvious immediate danger, nonintervention is often the best approach.

Wildlife organizations advise against attempting to care for young or injured animals yourself, as they require expert attention to stand the best chance of survival.

If in doubt, call your local wildlife rescue organization for advice.

Acknowledgments

There are many people without whom this book would not have been possible.

Thanks first to my brilliant agent, Natasha Fairweather, for her early belief and her expertise, and to everyone at RCW who worked to see this book published. Thanks, too, to my editor Lettice Franklin for her vision and her friendship. I'd also like to thank everyone at Orion who worked so hard in unusual circumstances to hatch this book into the world. Special thanks to Valerie Steiker and all at Scribner for their work on the American edition.

My greatest love and thanks to Janina Pedan for her love, support, and iron will.

Thanks also to Ksenia Pedan, who stumbled across a baby magpie one spring morning and decided to pick it up; China and Lily Williams for letting me into their lives and for giving me the space to write this book; Esther Samson, champion fly killer and grandmother; Romany Gilmour, wrangler of corpulent cats; Joe Gilmour for all his excellent advice about avian ailments; Gabriel Gilmour for his aviary-building skills; Jaz Rowland for her bird whispering; John Sutherland for "maggot pie"; Sarah Lee for her eyes; Rhik Samadder, god among pigeons; and Jim, wise egg. Love and gratitude to my parents, Polly and David, who have both juggled fire, and to all those who have been there for me through good and bad.

Thank to Louis Eliot for showing me around his family home, and to the trustees of the Eliot Estate for giving permission to reprint the words of Peregrine Eliot; to the members of staff in the reading rooms at the British Library and to Kathleen Shoemaker at the Stuart A. Rose Manuscript, Archives, and Rare Book Library at Emory University.

There are many writers whose works have been an inspiration. Thanks are due to Boria Sax for his writings on crows and culture; John Marzluff for his research into the existence of culture among crows and ravens; Lyanda Lynn Haupt for *Crow Planet*; Tim Birkhead for his detailed observations of the social lives of magpies; Esther Woolfson for her touching personal account of crow-habitation; Max Porter for the math-bomb motherfucker in *Grief Is the Thing with Feathers*; Robert Macfarlane for showing the hidden ways; and Helen Macdonald, in whose slipstream I can only hope to fly.

Thanks to the members of the corvid community for their generous advice and encouragement. And thanks to the magpie known as Benzene, who taught me more than she will ever know and who died of natural causes just before her fourth spring came into bloom.

Love beyond the sky to Olga Samson Pedan Gilmour, who uncovers hidden treasure every single day.

About the Author

Charlie Gilmour lives in South London with his wife and daughter.